CLEAN ENERGY AND RURAL DEVELOPMENT

SHIV | BIJAYA B. NAYAK | DEBASHREE | ADARSH | ANUP | SOUMYA | SASMITA | BONITA | AKANKSHYA | MONALISHA

Copyright © Shiv, Bijaya B. Nayak, Debashree, Adarsh, Anup, Soumya, Sasmita, Bonita, Akankshya, Monalisha

All Rights Reserved.

We owe a special debt to our parents who have been our
guiding spirit and taught us the value of integrity, humility
and sincerity. To them we respectfully dedicate this small
piece of work.

Authors of the Book

Contents

Contents

Foreword

India, a country where nearly 70% of country's population lives in rural areas, also a country where the emphasis is being given to clean energy and clean energy products since a few years now, needs to understand more about the rural development and progress on interventions related to clean energy and clean energy products in rural India.

There is huge market opportunity for clean energy products in rural economy of India. There is lot of innovation happening in the country, including research and development in the field of clean energy. State and Central Governments are making necessary changes in policies to promote clean energy sector. Educational institutes are also building Centres of Excellence for developing and innovating clean energy products. Incubation Centres are being set up by government and private bodies to encourage entrepreneurs.

This book gives an overview of clean energy in India and how the diffusion of clean energy products has happened in the rural parts of India since few years. It also highlights how entrepreneurial ecosystem and culture is being built in the field of clean energy. It shows few marketing models for the clean energy products in rural areas of Odisha. This book also covers the role of education in enhancing the quality of life of rural poor through clean energy, and also the role of consumer's education on eco-consumption. It also highlights the role of training and development that is required for the rural population through NGOs.

This book highlights the research and findings of few particular models that has been implemented in Southern

Odisha such as sustainable energy irrigation model, simulation of solar operated agri-pesticide, solar box type cooker, etc. It also showcases few case studies and its results to understand the impact of the innovations.

This book is a must read to understand the rural India in the context of the interventions being made in the field of clean energy, its progress and its impact.

Preface

Constantly increasing demand for energy that is solely based on unclean energy sources cannot be sustained indefinitely. The Earth's limited resources will soon run out. Energy is a critical component required for rural development, economic progress of a region or country and global well-being. The realisation that unclean energy sources are running out has pushed scientists, engineers, policy makers, etc. to look for alternative sources of energy that may supply, demand in the near and far future. It has been acknowledged that priority should be given to resources that are continuous, clean, and pollution-free. This book is devoted to comprehending these sources.

Acknowledgements

Many people have contributed to this book, and we owe our sincere gratitude to them. However, we are solely responsible for the shortcomings and possible errors. We are indebted to all persons who have contributed in some way or the other in getting our long-standing dream come to reality.

We are grateful to Mr. Gautam Kumar Pradhan, Regional Head of SELCO Foundation for Odisha and Jharkhand, for his exhaustive comments, and patience to remain attentive in many long discussions, supporting us in providing various reports, and other details during the making of this book.

We would like to express deep gratitude to Dr. Haribandhu Panda, Ex-VC, Centurion University of Technology and Management and Director of Klorofeel Foundation, Prof. Sashi Sekhar Garabadu, Chairman of Zenith Group of Institutions, Prof. Anup Padhi, Director of Zenith Group of Institutions and Dr. Sanjib Pattnaik, Principal of Zenith School of Management and our colleagues for their support and encouragement to complete this work. We would like to thank all our friends, well-wishers whose list is long enough to mention here for their encouragement and moral support.

Authors of the Book

Prologue

By the end of March 2017, less than 1 billion people in the world lacked access to electricity, while 2.7 billion lacked access to clean cooking energy (REN21, 2019). The majority of these individuals resided in underdeveloped Asian and Sub-Saharan African nations. India alone had 168 million people without power and 703 million without clean cooking energy.

The amount of clean energy used, a country's economic prosperity, and residents' quality of life are all inextricably intertwined. The degree of primary energy purity and the subsequent transformation process have substantial environmental repercussions in the form of global warming. As a result, in the energy transformation and value system, there is a need to change to low carbon clean energy. Such a system necessitates the availability of the suitable sort of clean energy, the appropriate product, process technology, user affordability and appropriate institutions.

This book comprises of various chapters related to clean energy and rural development. The findings of the chapters can help policy makers, marketing agencies and divisions of companies to understand clean energy, and it can help the unserved areas among poor consumers in a systematic way.

CHAPTER ONE

INTRODUCTION

Eliminating poverty and safeguarding sustainability are two of the most pressing issues of our day. Energy has the remedy to both. Increasing access to modern energy is vital to enabling human and economic development by directly providing energy services for basic requirements while also supporting productive uses and job creation. Access to contemporary energy services such as electricity, natural gas, and modern cooking fuel, among other things, is required for increased health and agricultural output.

Modern energy, in the form of electricity, has now become a significant component of the country's economic progress. Electrification is associated to a variety of development gains, such as increased income, job creation, and improved health and education. Electricity usage has skyrocketed in recent years. With an installed capacity of 367.28GW as of 2019, India is the world's third largest producer and third largest user of electricity (IBEF, 2018). During the fiscal year 2018-19, India produced 175000GWh of power, with coal accounting for 141137GWh, natural gas accounting for 23785GWh and oil accounting for 7723GWh. Electricity usage has increased dramatically, from 4182GWh in 1947 to 1196309GWh in

2019. (CEA, 2019). With increased demand for power and its generation from coal, there is fear that supplies of coal, petroleum, and other resources may be depleted. It also has a negative impact on the ecosystem. Greenhouse Gas (GHG) emissions are primarily responsible for environmental damage. In 2018, the world's GHG emissions from filthy energy sources were 36.83 billion tonnes (Bt) of carbon dioxide (CO_2), while India's GHG emissions totaled 2.57 Bt of CO_2 (Tollefson, 2019).

In the perspective of delivering contemporary energy services to everybody, these are not convincing criteria. There is a need to transition from using unclean energy sources to using clean energy sources. Clean energy is defined as any energy source or form that does not cause negative externalities when consumed. Energy obtained from the sun, wind, water, and waves is referred to as clean energy since it emits relatively low greenhouse gas. Furthermore, energy derived from coal, petroleum, and other fossil fuels is referred to as filthy energy.

India must expand its clean energy base to meet the demands of its people, as well as create a mandate for the provision of increasing the percentage of clean energy in the total energy mix. The utilisation of clean energy, both centralised and distributed, is the way ahead for obtaining a higher quality of life.

Any effort to meet people's energy requirements with inconsistent electricity, via centralised grid-based power generation with its transmission and distribution concerns, would worsen the situation. To solve the problem, a number of social entrepreneurs are focusing their efforts on last-mile energy supply. There is a chance for the country's underserved population to bypass the grid and adopt dependable, decentralised clean energy alternatives.

The establishment of a supporting ecosystem is required to facilitate the implementation of such solutions. A recent research was conducted to examine the various providers of sustainable energy products in India. It was determined that a robust ecosystem with increased information flow is required in order for the dissemination of clean energy goods to occur swiftly in India. An ecosystem like this can encourage large-scale replication of clean energy solutions.

1.1 Rationale

Energy demand is proportional to economic progress (UNDP, 2001). Adoption of clean energy has the potential to improve global GDP by 2.5 percent by 2050. In addition to economic development, providing the availability of dependable clean energy solutions at an accessible price has become critical in order to lessen the destructive effects of fossil fuels on the environment and enhance people's quality of life. Their use, however, is limited. Its limited applications might be owing to insufficient institutional frameworks for affordable finance and supply chain difficulties. People in rural regions confront concerns such as poor quality of life, low income, and energy-related issues such as availability, dependability, affordability, cost, drudgery, pollution, safety, and health-related issues. As a result, a clean energy infrastructure that can solve these difficulties in a sustainable way is required. All choices, from upfront acquisition of a clean energy system to becoming an enabling device for revenue creation, must be investigated. Sustainable energy-powered livelihoods are vary in character. It might include agricultural, manufacturing, and service sectors that are contextually distinct in diverse topographies. As a result, technological, financial, and delivery model changes are required for economic and quality-of-life development. Many research on technology dissemination have been conducted due to its importance.

1.2 Chapter Plan

This book contains twelve chapters. The first chapter is about introduction and rationale. The second chapter gives an overview on clean energy in India. Third chapter focuses on the concept of clean energy, demand for clean energy products, factors affecting diffusion of clean energy products, marketing of products in rural areas and difficulty in diffusion of clean energy products in rural areas. Chapter fourth gives emphasis on entrepreneurial eco-system. Chapter five covers role of education in enhancing quality of life of rural people. Sixth chapter focuses on the impact of consumer's education on eco-consumption. Seventh chapter covers role of training and development for rural people. Chapter eight focuses on marketing models for clean energy products in rural areas of Odisha. Chapter nine covers sustainable energy irrigation model for enhancing livelihood security in rural areas of South Odisha. Tenth chapter emphasis on a clean energy product called solar operated agri-pesticide sprayer and eleventh chapter on solar operated box type cooker. Lastly twelveth chapter focuses on some case study from South Odisha accompanied with some recommendations.

CHAPTER TWO

CLEAN ENERGY IN INDIA: AN OVERVIEW

This chapter focuses on development of different clean energy or renewable energy policies, initiatives, undertaken in India. This chapter has three section. The first section, focuses on clean energy access framework. Second section gives a global overview on clean energy. Later it speaks about the evolution of Indian power sector and the clean energy development policies in our country and the last section focuses on the diffusion of solar lights across the various districts of Odisha in India.

The biggest difficulties in today's world are putting an end to poverty and embracing sustainability. Energy is the answer to both problems. Electricity, as a kind of energy, has now become a significant feature in the country's economic growth. Access to electricity creates barriers in the development of livelihoods, employment, access to health, industry, and education, and has a detrimental influence on economic growth and living standards. The demand for power has skyrocketed in recent years. Today, our country is the world's third largest producer and third greatest user of power (BP Report, 2016). During the fiscal year (FY) 2019-20, utilities in India generated 1383.5 TWh of gross electricity, whereas total power generation (utilities and non-utilities) in the country was 1598 TWh. With increased demand for power and its generation from coal, there is fear that supplies of coal, petroleum, and other resources may be depleted. It also has a negative impact on the ecosystem. Every year, 8 billion metric tonnes of carbon enter our atmosphere, with fossil fuels accounting for 6.5 billion tonnes and deforestation accounting for 1.5 billion tonnes. India's energy industry contributed significantly to the country's greenhouse gas (GHG) emissions and is heavily reliant on fossil fuels. Both are not particularly appealing standards in the context of ensuring universal access to high-quality power. To be sustainable in the future, there is a need to transition away from traditional energy sources and toward renewable energy. Our country requires more energy to support its growing population, as well as a provision to raise the amount of renewables in the total energy mix. Clean energy generated through the usage of decentralised products is the solution.

Clean energy, also called renewable energy, is a major concern for the government, market, civil society, and individuals throughout the country, but particularly in Eastern India. The government is now directing its attention to the Eastern part of India in order to encourage the use of clean energy.

2.1 Framework for Clean Energy Access

Access to clean energy is critical for human growth. An attempt has been made to devise a framework for clean energy access. Many elements are responsible for clean energy access, but the bulk of them may be classified as financing, capacity building, infrastructure, technology, and policy making, all of which are required for rural energy access. In terms of financing, it includes access to the product's final consumer. The existence of Self Help Groups (SHGs) and cooperative societies must assist the end users in obtaining loans. These businesses should be linked to financial institutions so that end users can receive funds for additional loans. The presence of banks and microcredit agencies in the region, as well as their ability to distribute funds, are critical elements in process spread.

In terms of capacity building, elements such as product knowledge, technical training, and assistance for product operation and maintenance will help the end-users to gain access to clean energy. Other important factors include, government and private training institutions, support centres, the presence of local NGOs, and so on. These activities help in generating awareness about the need for and use of clean energy at the household, livelihood, and community levels, which is required for end-users to have access to clean energy. Energy is essential for infrastructure growth in schools, community centres, health centres, and other places. It may also aid in the construction of communication networks, highways, and other soft support units.

From a technological prespective, the presence of dependable local vendors and suppliers, as well as the development of a strong supply network with inexpensive high-quality goods, technologies, spare parts, and appliances, would aid in the availability of clean energy to end-users. Furthermore, a robust labour force with technical expertise helps assure the seamless operation and functionality of the items. From a policy prespective, it focuses on present, possible objectives, guidelines, schemes available, and so on, which will aid in addressing clean energy access. If the system components can be found locally, produced, and installed, it will establish an environment for the diffusion of clean energy products. This will aid in the creation of jobs, reduction of costs, provision of speedier service, and development of local capability. Figure 2.1 shows the framework for energy access.

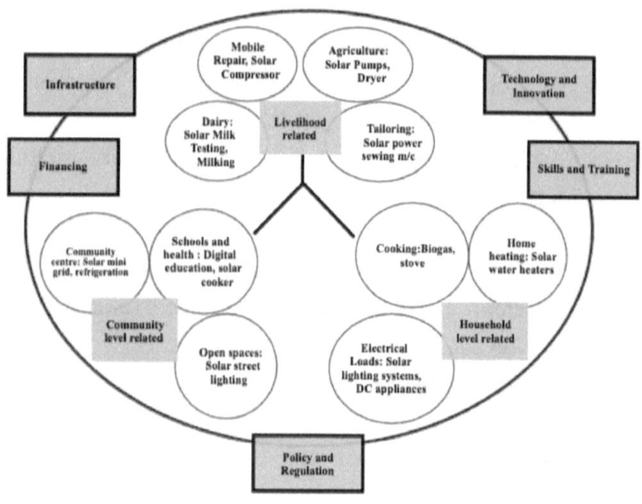

Figure 2.1: Framework for Energy Access

2.1.1 Clean Energy: A Global Overview

Clean energy is expected to provide around 35 percent (percent) of global energy consumption in 2022-23 and 27 percent in 2019. Renewables accounted for over 40 percent of global power generation growth in 2016, and 31 percent of global primary energy growth. Around 162GW of renewable energy was added in 2016-17, resulting in a hefty annual gain of 9 percent as compared to 2015-16. Solar Photovoltaics (PV) provided for 47 percent of newly built renewable power capacity, while hydropower and wind accounted for around 16 and 34 percent, respectively. As a result, renewables were anticipated to account for 62 percent of net additions to worldwide power producing capacity in 2016-17.

By the end of 2017, global renewable energy capacity has increased by 167GW, reaching roughly 2179GW. Solar PV has increased by 32 percent in 2017, while wind energy has decreased by 10 percent. Underpinning this rise are significant cost reductions, with the levelized price of energy from solar PV falling by 73 percent and onshore wind falling by roughly one-quarter between 2010 and 2017.

2.1.2 Market Review on Solar PV: World Wide

In 2016-17, total solar PV installed capacity surpassed 300GW, with China accounting for 34.5GW, followed by the United States with 14.5GW, Japan with 10.2GW, and India in fourth position with 5GW. In India, around 79GW of capacity was projected to be installed during the 2017-18 fiscal year. In an attempt to maintain ongoing growth, around 8.8GW of capacity development (a 76 percent increase over 2016) was planned to make China the third largest PV market in 2017, surpassing Japan. Prices for solar modules are continuing to decline at a rapid pace. In the first quarter of 2017-18, prices in India plummeted to less than one dollar, which is comparable to Rs 45 to 72/Wp depending on the brand and firm. As a result of this rapid decline, solar PV has become an inexpensive new source of electricity in the majority of countries, as well as a boon to rising economies.

2.2 India: Clean Energy Potential, Targets and Achievements

2.2.1 Clean Energy Potential

India has the greatest potential for renewable energy generation. It accounts for around 4 percent of global power output and contributes 4.43 percent of global renewable generating capacity. According to the International Energy Agency (IEA), clean energy supply will increase to 4550GW globally by 2040.

By 2018, our country's total installed clean electricity generation capacity was at 114.32GW, accounting for 33.23 percent of the overall installed capacity of 344GW. From 2008 to 2018, installed clean power production capacity expanded at a CAGR of 9.29 percent. During the fiscal year 2017-18, India installed a record 11788MW of clean energy capacity. In 2018, clean energy generated 93.21 billion units of power. The Government of India has set a target of achieving a total capacity of 175GW from different clean energy sources by 2022-23. 100 GW is from solar electricity, 60 GW is from hydro power, 10 GW is from biomass power, and 5 GW is from small hydro power. Since the commencement of the National Biogas and Manure Management Programme (NBMMP) in March 2010, about 5058054 biogas plant units have been established in India. Table 2.1 summarises our country's clean energy potential per state as of December 2017.

Table 2.1: State-wise Clean Energy Potential in the Country in MW till 2017

Sl. No	State/UT	Wind Power	Small Hydro Power	Biomass Power	Biogasse Cogeneration	Waste to Energy	Solar	Total
1	Andhra Pradesh	14497	978	578	300	123	38440	54916
2	Arunanchal Pradesh	236	1341	8	0	0	8650	10235
3	Assam	112	239	212	0	8	13760	14331
4	Bihar	144	223	619	300	73	11200	12559
5	Chattisgarh	314	1107	236	0	24	18270	19951
6	Delhi	0	0	0	0	131	2050	2181
7	Goa	0	7	26	0	0	880	913
8	Gujarat	35071	202	1221	350	112	35770	72726
9	Haryana	93	110	1333	350	24	4560	6470

Sl. No	State/UT	Wind Power	Small Hydro Power	Biomass Power	Biogasse Cogeneration	Waste to Energy	Solar	Total
10	Himachal Pradesh	64	2398	142	0	2	33840	36446
11	Jammu and Kashmir	5685	1431	43	0	0	111050	118209
12	Jharkhand	91	209	90	0	10	18180	18580
13	Karnataka	13593	4141	1131	450	0	24700	44015
14	Kerela	837	704	1044	0	36	6110	8731
15	Madhya Pradesh	2931	820	1364	0	78	61660	66853
16	Maharastra	5961	794	1887	1250	287	64320	74499
17	Manipur	56	109	13	0	2	10630	10810
18	Meghalaya	82	230	11	0	2	5860	6185
19	Mizoram	0	169	1	0	2	9090	9262
20	Nagaland	16	197	10	0	0	7290	7513
21	Odisha	1384	295	246	0	22	25780	27727
22	Punjab	0	441	3172	300	45	2810	6768
23	Rajasthan	5050	57	1039	0	62	142310	148518
24	Sikim	98	267	2	0	0	4940	5307
25	Tamil Nadu	14152	660	1070	450	151	17670	34153
26	Telengana	0	0	0	0	0	20410	20410
27	Tripura	0	47	3	0	2	2080	2132
28	Uttar Pradesh	1260	461	1617	1250	176	22830	27594
29	Uttarakhand	534	1708	24	0	5	16800	19071
30	West Bengal	22	396	396	0	148	6260	7222
31	Chandigarh	0	0	0	0	6	0	6
32	Andaman and Nicobar	365	8	0	0	0	0	373
33	Lakshadeep	0	0	0	0	0	0	0
34	Puducherry	120	0	0	0	3	0	123
35	Daman and Diu	4	0	0	0	0	0	4
36	Others	0	0	0	0	1022	790	1812
	TOTAL	102772	19749	17536	5000	2554	748990	896605

Source: MNRE, 2017 (Others: Include other State)

Source: MNRE, 2017 (Others: Include other State)

From table 3.1, it is evident that Rajasthan is having the largest potential for clean energy and solar energy, followed Jammu and Kashmir, Maharastra and Gujarat. Odisha stands at 10th position with a total clean energy potential of 27727 MW in the year 2016-17 and 8th position with 25780

MW for potential of solar power.

2.3 Clean Targets and Achievements

India has set a goal of achieving 175GW from clean energy sources by 2022-23. Because solar is expected to meet the majority of the objective, 60GW is set aside for ground-mounted, grid-connected big solar projects, with another 40GW put aside for rooftop solar. Due to climatic circumstances, additional objectives have been given to the southern region with 59GW, 54GW to the western region, and 46GW to the northern region. Overall, it is projected to install more than 90 percent of the overall objectives set, with the remainder coming from the north-eastern and eastern areas. If the 175GW objective is met, it will contribute to achieving 19.44 percent of the overall clean energy potential of 900GW. The western Indian state of Maharashtra has set a lofty aim of 22 GW, followed by Tamil Nadu with 21.5 GW. Odisha has set a goal of achieving 2.3 GW of clean energy by 2022-23.

2.3.1 Generation from Clean Energy

Electricity generation from clean energy is growing year after year. As of March 2020, over 36 percent of India's installed electrical generation capacity comes from clean energy, which generates approximately 21 percent of total utility electricity in our country (All India Installed Capacity of Power Stations).

2.3.2 Off-Grid Decentralised Solar PV Program

Clean energy, whether in an off-grid decentralised or independent mode, is an ideal, scalable, and sustainable alternative for delivering electricity to un-electrified, power-deficient towns and hamlets in rural locations. The Ministry is providing Central Financial Assistance (CFA) to implementing agencies under the off-grid decentralised solar PV programme for the fiscal year 2017-18 for the diffusion of solar photovoltaic (SPV) home lighting systems, solar street lights, solar pumps, power packs, and other solar applications to meet the electricity and lighting needs of individuals in rural areas. The major implementing agency through which CFA of 30 percent is supplied is the State Nodal Agency (SNA). NABARD is one of the implementing agencies for pumps and lighting systems, providing CFA at 40 percent of the benchmark cost. Table 2.2 shows the state-by-state installation of off-grid solar systems in India until December 2020.

Table 2.2: State wise Installation of Off-Grid Solar Systems till Dec 2020

Sl. No	State/UT	Solar Home Lights	Solar Lamps	Solar Street Lights	Solar Pumps	Solar Power Plant (kW)
1	Andhra Pradesh	22972	77803	15468	34045	3815.59
2	Arunanchal Pradesh	35065	76401	13741	22	963.2
3	Assam	46879	647761	16338	45	1605
4	Bihar	12303	1735227	46032	2813	6800
5	Chattisgarh	42232	3311	2792	61970	31372.9
6	Delhi	0	4807	301	90	1269

Sl. No	State/UT	Solar Home Lights	Solar Lamps	Solar Street Lights	Solar Pumps	Solar Power Plant (kW)
7	Goa	393	1093	707	15	32.7
8	Gujarat	9253	31603	5004	11522	13576.6
9	Haryana	56727	93853	34625	5014	2321.25
10	Himachal Pradesh	22592	33909	92500	15	1905.5
11	Jammu & Kashmir	144316	51224	22900	39	8129.85
12	Jharkhand	9450	790515	13572	4800	3769.9
13	Karnataka	52638	7781	5069	7435	7854.01
14	Kerela	41912	54367	1735	818	16048.39
15	Madhya Pradesh	7920	529101	13611	23156	3654
16	Maharastra	3497	239297	10420	11315	3857.7
17	Manipur	24583	9058	22217	40	1580.5
18	Meghalaya	14874	40750	5800	19	2004
19	Mizoram	12060	91201	10117	37	3885
20	Nagaland	1045	6766	11107	3	1506
21	Odisha	5274	99843	17815	9599	2191.515
22	Punjab	8626	17495	43448	4663	2066
23	Rajasthan	187968	225851	7114	53423	30449
24	Sikim	15059	23300	504	0	850
25	Tamil Nadu	298641	16818	39908	6289	13052.6
26	Telengana	0	0	1958	424	7450
27	Tripura	32723	253443	6284	151	867
28	Uttar Pradesh	235909	2346365	289355	29600	10638.31
29	Uttarakhand	91595	163386	31535	26	4059.53
30	West Bengal	145332	17662	15302	653	1730
31	Andaman and Nicobar	468	6296	920	5	167
32	Chandigarh	275	1675	901	12	730
33	Lakshadeep	600	5289	4465	0	2190
34	Puducherry	25	1637	417	21	121
36	Others	24047	125797	9150	609	23885
37	NABARD (2015 onwards)	116226	0	0	4012	0
	TOTAL	1723479	7830685	813132	272700	216398.7

Source: MNRE, 2020

From table 2.2 it is found that maximum number of the solar home lights were installed in Tamil Nadu, followed by Uttar Pradesh and Rajasthan. A total of 122932 number of solar home lights, solar lamps and solar street lights have been installed till Dec 2020-21.

2.4 Policy Landscape on Clean Energy in India

Electricity is an absolute need in all facets of our lives. It is a must. It is a precarious infrastructure on which India's socio-economic progress is predicated. Recognizing that energy is one of the key drivers of rapid economic growth and helps in poverty reduction, our government has established a goal of providing complete access to power to all homes. In addition, a target was set for bringing dependable and high-quality power to rural India at an affordable cost, which is a critical prerequisite for overall development and prosperity. The next sub-section focuses on different clean energy policies.

2.4.1 Evolution of Renewable Power Sector and Renewable Energy Development Policies

The emergence of renewable power occurred mostly after 2003, with the passage of the Electricity Act of 2003. Three main measures were implemented, laying the groundwork for India's renewable energy growth. Some of the policies include National Electricity Policy 2005, National Rural Electrification Policies 2006, and National Tariff Policy 2006. The Electricity Act of 2003 was further revised to create programmes like as the Deen Dayal Upadhyaya Gram Jyoti Yojana (DDUGJY) and the Rajiv Gandhi Grameen Vidyutikaran Yojana (RGGVY) to electrify all villages. In 2006, the National Tariff Policy was implemented to acquire a set amount of grid-based power from renewable energy sources. Furthermore, the establishment of the National Action Plan on Climate Change (NAPCC) paved the door for the creation of eight missions to deal with climate change adaptation and mitigation.

The first phase of energy policy was implemented before 1956, when the Electricity Supply Act was introduced and the foundation of semi-autonomous State

Electricity Boards (SEBs) was legislated. Second phase, was implemented from 1956 and 1991. Here, the ownership of electricity generation and distribution was transferred to the state, and emphasis was given on reducing power losses, subsidies, and infrastructure bottlenecks. The third phase was the Liberalisation phase, which lasted from 1991 to 2003. It witnessed the introduction of provisions for private sector participation in generation, as well as fast track clearing mechanisms for private investment proposals. Finally, the fourth phase focused on the introduction of the Electricity Regulatory Commissions Act in 1998, which led to the establishment of central and state electricity regulatory commissions as well as tariff rationalisation.

2.4.2 Electricity Act 2003

This act paved the way for the advancement and integration of renewable energy into the grid. The overarching goal was to familiarise competition, safeguard consumer interests, and offer power to everybody. This policy directs the State Electricity Regulatory Commissions (SERCs) to encourage renewable and non-conventional energy sources under their authority. A proportion for purchasing electricity from these sources was made operable for the promotional rates defined by the individual SERCs. The proportion of power derived from renewable energy sources has gradually grown, as mandated by SERCs. Distribution businesses must make such purchases through a competitive bidding procedure.

2.4.3 National Electricity Policy 2005

This policy acknowledges that electricity is a necessary element for survival. The goal of this programme was to offer power to everyone by 2010, to meet demand completely by 2012, and to go for reserves after meeting peak requirements. The key goals of this programme was to increase per capita availability to above 1000 kWh per year by 2012 and to ensure a minimum lifeline use of 365 kWh per year per family by 2012.

2.4.4 National Rural Electrification Policies (NREP), 2006

The goal of this programme was to have access to quality and consistent power supply at reasonable rates by 2012, with a minimal lifeline use of one unit/household/day. It was also said that in villages/habitations where grid access was neither practical or cost viable, off-grid clean energy products based on stand-alone clean energy based systems will be used for power delivery. If it was not practicable, lighting sources such as solar photovoltaic would be used, but these houses would not be classified as electrified. The plan was prepared by the state government and would be connected to a district-level development plan engaging the Gram Panchayat (GP). The first certificate was to be issued by the village gramme panchayat when the village becomes eligible for declaration as electrified. Following that, the gramme panchayat must declare and affirm the village's electrified status as of March 31st of each year.

2.4.5 National Tariff Policy 2006

There was a clause in this legislation that required the national and state electrical regulatory bodies to acquire a specific amount of grid-based power from renewable energy sources. State Electricity Regulatory Commissions will require distribution licensees to meet a Renewable Energy Purchase Obligation (RPO) within a certain time frame. Purchase commitments were given to each state, with 0.25 percent of power purchases by states by 2013 and 3 percent by 2022.

Renewable Energy Purchase Obligation objectives can be met after the Green Energy Corridor (a transmission network connecting clean energy-rich states to energy-deficient ones) is completed, since it will allow for easier trading in clean energy electricity. MNRE's new rooftop policy is also expected to boost installation activity in the sector (helping with RPO obligations). Odisha has a lower solar RPO (of 0.15 percent in 2012-13) than the 0.25 percent objective set in the pricing programme for 2014-15. With a rise in the proportion of total energy consumption in Odisha, the power to be harvested from solar climbed from 44MU to 210MU, with a growth rate of 48 percent in 2015-16.

2.4.6 Off-grid, Decentralised Solar Power Schemes

Technically, this initiative supported off-grid, decentralised PV systems and mini-grids for rural electrification up to a maximum capacity of 500 kWp per site. This approach was applied by a number of implementing agencies in order to achieve quick upscaling in an inclusive manner. This plan provides financial help in the form of a 30 percent capital subsidy to end-users and a 90 percent subsidy to special category states for community initiatives and government agencies for the construction of solar PV systems. It also provided a credit-linked capital subsidy plan through NABARD, other regional rural banks, and commercial banks for solar illumination and pumping purposes. The government gave a 30 percent subsidy on the cost of the system, which ranged from Rs 21-105 per watt peak depending on the capacity of the modules and the layout of the solar photovoltaic systems in various areas of the nation. The capital subsidy for solar water pumping systems ranges from Rs 27630 to 57600 per/hp, depending on the capacity.

2.4.7 Jawaharlal Nehru National Solar Mission (JNNSM)

JNNSM was established in 2008 as part of India's National Action Plan on Climate Change (NAPCC). It seeks to develop our nation as a global leader in solar energy by fostering a favourable legislative environment for its widespread deployment. The initial 2010 plan was to reach a total installed solar capacity of 20GW by 2022. The aims were divided into three phases, with phase I lasting from 2010 to 2013, phase II lasting from 2013 to 2017, and phase III lasting from 2017 to 2022. Each phase consisted of three segments: solar rooftop, off-grid solar applications, and solar collectors; phase-I aimed at 1100MW, 200MW, and 7 million square metres, respectively. Similarly, phase II aimed at 10000MW, 1000MW, and 15 million square metres, respectively, while the targets for phase III aimed at 20000MW, 2000MW, and 20 million square metres. The government raised the solar target for 2022 from 20GW to 100GW once again. For 2015-16, 2016-17, 2017-18, 2018-19, 2019-2020, and 2021-2022, the revised objectives were 5000MW, 17000MW, 32000MW, 48000MW, 65000MW, 82500MW, and 100000MW.

2.5 Diffusion of Solar Home Lights in Odisha

The state of Odisha is attempting to electrify villages. By the end of March 31, 2017, 95 percent of Odisha's 51582 villages had been electrified. In Odisha, a total of 34216 solar lights were installed. Odisha Renewable Energy Development Authority (OREDA) built 14837 solar lights in rural households (HH) in the state of Odisha during the fiscal year 2017-18. Odisha plans to generate 2200 MW of solar power, 200 MW of wind power, 180 MW of biomass power, 150 MW of small hydro power, and 20 MW of waste-to-energy (WTE) electricity by 2022.

2.5.1 District-wise Diffusion of Solar Home Lights across the state of Odisha.

Table 2.3 shows the district wise diffusion of solar lights across Odisha.

Table 2.3: Diffusion of Solar Home Lights in Odisha

Districts	Rural HH	Urban HH	Total HH	No of Solar Home Light Installed in Urban HH	No of Solar Home Light Installed in Rural HH	Total Number of Solar Home Light Installed (2011 Census)	Solar Home Lights Installed for Urban Household	Solar Home Lights installed for total household (per 1000 HH)	Solar Home Lights installed per rural household (per 1000)
Angul	249585	46337	295922	97	902	999	2.09	3.38	3.61
Balasore	473512	55895	529407	89	1804	1893	1.59	3.58	3.81
Bargarh	339364	34027	373391	46	826	872	1.35	2.34	2.43
Bhadrak	274191	35336	309527	85	842	927	2.41	2.99	3.07
Boudh	103239	4488	107727	10	273	283	2.23	2.63	2.64
Bolangir	387345	44736	432081	117	1504	1621	2.62	3.75	3.88
Cuttack	425082	141749	566831	153	922	1075	1.08	1.90	2.17
Debgarh	70511	5431	75942	7	240	247	1.29	3.25	3.40
Dhenkanal	253118	25252	278370	16	434	450	0.63	1.62	1.71
Gajapati	112872	15946	128818	17	468	485	1.07	3.77	4.15
Ganjam	602216	154678	756894	223	1444	1667	1.44	2.20	2.40
Jajpur	378135	29437	407572	42	994	1036	1.43	2.54	2.63
Jagatsingpur	237411	28177	265588	99	1045	1144	3.51	4.31	4.40
Jharsuguda	83664	50960	134624	46	200	246	0.90	1.83	2.39
Kalahandi	377001	27813	404814	76	3344	3420	2.73	8.45	8.87
Kandhamal	155335	16669	172004	22	743	765	1.32	4.45	4.78
Kendrapara	311465	15940	327405	20	1379	1399	1.25	4.27	4.43
Keonjhar	349736	56893	406629	85	1937	2022	1.49	4.97	5.54
Khordha	247940	241696	489636	420	512	932	1.74	1.90	2.07
Koraput	283522	54683	338205	83	1467	1550	1.52	4.58	5.17
Malkangiri	126306	11144	137450	30	961	991	2.69	7.21	7.61
Mayurbhanj	544764	42884	587648	52	1526	1578	1.21	2.69	2.80
Nabarangapur	253461	20202	273663	39	1541	1580	1.93	5.77	6.08
Nayagarh	213265	17703	230968	21	936	957	1.19	4.14	4.39
Nuapada	151921	8026	159947	16	1116	1132	1.99	7.08	7.35
Puri	317002	52480	369482	60	803	863	1.14	2.34	2.53
Rayagada	191615	34349	225964	41	847	888	1.19	3.93	4.42
Sambalpur	178958	69871	248829	75	366	441	1.07	1.77	2.05
Sundargarh	310762	162531	473293	245	2197	2442	1.51	5.16	7.07
Subarnapur	140714	11740	152454	14	297	311	1.19	2.04	2.11
TOTAL	8144012	1517073	9661085	2346	31870	34216	1.55	3.54	3.91

Source: Census 2011

Source: Census 2011

Table 2.3 it was found that maximum number of solar lights were installed in Kalahandi district, followed by Sundargarh district and Kheonjhar district with 3420, 2442 and 2022 numbers respectively. Further it was found that a maximum of 0.84 percent of solar lights were installed in Kalahandi district, followed by Malkangiri with 0.72 percent.

2.6 Conclusion

The state of Odisha is attempting to electrify villages. By the end of March 31, 2017, 95 percent of Odisha's 51582 villages had been electrified. In Odisha, a total of 34216 solar lights were installed (ibid). Odisha Renewable Energy Development Authority (OREDA) built 14837 solar lights in rural households (HH) in the state of Odisha during the fiscal year 2017-18. Odisha plans to generate 2200 MW of solar power, 200 MW of wind power, 180 MW of bio-mass power, 150 MW of small hydro power, and 20 MW of waste-to-energy (WTE) electricity by 2022. The fundamental difficulty that we are currently experiencing is a lack of a solid foundation of numerous variables and players that supports the functioning and delivers long-term solutions. Moving on to the next chapter, it focuses on clean energy and diffusion of clean energy products in rural areas.

CHAPTER THREE

CLEAN ENERGY AND DIFFUSION OF CLEAN ENERGY PRODUCTS IN RURAL AREAS

This chapter focuses on clean energy, demand for clean energy, factors affecting diffusion of clean energy products, marketing of products in rural areas and difficulty in diffusion of clean energy products in rural areas. This chapter has five sections. The first section provides an overview on clean energy and clean energy products. Second section highlights on demand for clean energy products and section three focuses on characteristics of rural consumer. Fourth section focuses on marketing of products and services in rural areas and the last section focuses on the difficulty in diffusion of clean energy products in rural areas.

3.1 Clean Energy

According to Oxford Dictionary, energy means "power derived from the utilisation of physical or chemical resources, especially to provide light and heat or to work machines". The word energy is derived from the Greek word 'energon', which means 'in-work' or 'work content'. The work output depends on the energy input. Any activity carried out, whether by humans or by nature is mainly caused due to flow of energy in one form or the other. Julius Robert Mayer in 1842 discovered the law of conservation of energy, which is now called first law of thermodynamics, "Energy neither can be created nor be destroyed".

The energy sources can be classified in different ways. It includes primary and secondary energy, commercial and non-commercial energy and clean and unclean energy. Primary energy is found in nature. Example of primary energy sources include coal, oil, natural gas and biomass. When primary energy is converted, it results in secondary energy. Example of secondary energy sources include steam, electricity, etc. Commercial energy is the energy sources that are traded in the market. Example of commercial energy sources include coal, oil, natural gas and electricity. Energy sources that are not traded in the market, are called non-commercial energy. Example of non-commercial energy sources include biomass, solar, wind, etc.

There is no uniformly accepted definition of clean energy. Although it is referred to many renewable energy sources, petroleum products and electricity. For the purpose of present study, the "clean energy" is defined as that energy source or form which when used does not produce negative externalities. As an example, electricity when used at household level for cooking does not produce noxious gases like that from wood or coal or kerosene. Hence, electricity is a clean energy and wood, coal and kerosene are unclean energy. The production of clean energy may use processes with varying degree of cleanliness. For example, electricity produced from coal follows many unclean processes including coal mining, transportation, coal handling at the power plant, burning of coal, flue gas emission, ash disposal, etc. Whereas electricity produced from solar energy, wind energy, hydro energy, etc. do not have such unclean processes. It is often useful to distinguish end-use energy and its history of transformation for allocations clean/unclean energy. Through energy and product life cycle analysis one can rank them on a cleanliness scale. The energy form and products during its lifespan that generates highest amount of pollutants can be called most unclean and that produces least amount of pollutants can be ranked as most clean.

There are different products which use clean energy for cooking, transforming energy, etc. Clean energy products are "multiple variety of products, that uses clean materials and energy sources, which dramatically reduces the utilisation of natural resources and eliminating emissions and wastes" (Clean Edge, 2011). Use of clean energy products help in creating new avenues for earning, reduces cost, reduces drudgery and improves health conditions, thus helping in enhancing quality of life in rural areas (ibid). Clean energy products are associated with services.

Services include installation, repair and maintenance of the clean energy product. For example, installation of a solar based lighting system, training services is provided on how to operate, maintain and repair the product.

There are different clean energy products available. These include biomass cook stove, biogas plant, biomass gasifier, electric stove, Piped Natural Gas (PNG), Liquefied Petroleum Gas (LPG), solar based lighting systems, solar based irrigation systems, etc. These clean products can be classified based on CO2 emission. Table 3.1 gives the classification of clean energy products based on CO2 emission.

Table 3.1: Classification of Clean Energy Products on the Basis of CO_2 Emission

Clean Energy Products	Annual fuel quantity / useful energy	CO_2 Emission	CH_4 (ton CO_2 eq.)	N_2O (ton CO_2 eq.)	CO (ton CO_2 eq.)	Annual CO_2 eq. emissions (ton)
• **Biomass cook stoves**						
• Natural draft	3276 MJ	NA	0.08	0.04	0	0.32
• Forced draft using wood	3276 MJ	NA	0.08	0.04	0	0.22
• Forced draft using pellets	3276 MJ	NA	0.08	0.04	0	0.20
• **Biogas plant**	3276 MJ	0.47	0.01	0.01	0	0.48
• **Biomass gasifier**	125-150 Mt	0	0	0	0	0
• **Electric stove**	1320 kWh	1.21	NA	NA	NA	1.21
• Induction stove	1080 kWh	1.06	NA	NA	NA	1.06
• **PNG**	4851 SCF	0.26	0	0	NA	0.26
• **LPG**	3276 MJ	0.41	0	0	0	0.42
• **Solar based lighting system**	0	0	0	0	0	0
• **Solar based irrigation system**	0	0	0	0	0	0

Source: Jain et al. 2015; Bond et al. 2013; Mahapatra et al. 2009

The induction stove and others that use electricity for cooking produce more CO2 than coal and wood because of the way electricity is generated and used. Although electricity on its own is cleaner than coal and wood but when one considers the entire value chain, it becomes unclean. Hence, one must consider the source of electricity to rate the extent of cleanliness. For example, electricity produced from solar photovoltaic (PV) is cleaner than what produced from coal, wood and cleaner than energy used directly from coal and wood.

A brief description is given for different clean energy products available in rural areas.

3.1.1 Biomass Cook Stoves

Biomass cook stove is a combustion device that burns biomass fuel. With advancement of technology and growing concern for energy security and health hazard concern for women and children in rural areas efficient biomass cook stove helps in reducing emissions and offers cleaner cooking energy solutions. It is primarily fuelled through firewood and uses processed pelletised fuel. Use of advanced biomass cook stove produces heat energy through combustion which is transferred to food or is lost to the surrounding (Jetter et al. 2012). Biomass is freely available, and more than 70 percent of biomass consumption in rural households is commercially procured (Jain et al. 2015). Biomass cook stoves are classified based on "air augmentation inside the combustion chamber" as natural and force draft. Natural draft biomass cook stove improves combustion efficiency due to its geometry, design and insulating material as compared to traditional cook stove. The thermal efficiency ranges from 25 to 30 percent. Forced draft biomass cook stove uses a fan for supplying air into the combustion chamber making it more efficient compared to natural draft biomass cook stove. The thermal efficiency ranges from 35 to 40 percent. As per Unnat Chulha Abhiyan, a program by Government of India (GoI), about 2.75 million improved biomass cook stoves for household and community will be installed (MNRE, 2017). Use of biomass cook stove leads to increase in efficiency, has less operating cost, requires low maintenance and is inexpensive fuel source (ibid).

3.1.2 Household and Community based Biogas Plant

Biogas plant is another important clean energy product available, which satisfies the needs for rural consumers in India. Biogas is a clean, non-polluting, smokeless domestic fuel mainly used in rural areas in India. It contains 55 to 75 percent Methane Gas (CH4) and has a high calorific value. It is produced from cattle dung, human excreta and other organic waste generated from home and surroundings. Biogas is produced through anaerobic digestion in the biogas plant. It reduces the use of wood, helps in improving health, sanitation and other environmental conditions. It is available in low cost and is simple to use. It is a clean and convenient fuel used for cooking in rural households. Biogas has gained popularity in India and is the largest and most prominent of all rural clean energy technology implemented by the government (Ramana, 1991). Biomass contributes over a third of primary energy in India and is predominantly used in rural households for cooking, heating etc. (NCAER, 1992). About 4.8 million biogas plants have been installed in India till 2016 (MNRE and IPNG Statistics Report, 2017).

3.1.3 Biomass Gasifier

Biomass gasifier is another clean energy product which uses the gasification technology. According to The Energy and Resources Institute (TERI), biomass gasification is a method of conversion of solid biomass fuel to producer gas through a sequence of thermo-chemical reactions. The producer gas can be used for cooking purpose both at household, community and institutional level. Since the gas contains Carbon Monoxide (CO), it has to be cautiously handled at household level. Some safety measures like addition of additives which can warn in case of gas leakage can be carried out. Biomass is used as fuel which reduces the need for fossil fuel. It is available from agricultural waste. Growing biomass crops produces oxygen and helps reducing carbon dioxide emission. It is a mature technology available in several designs ranging from small to modular type. It is operated in a decentralised manner, flexible and economically viable for power generation. It also helps in generating employment. About 0.2 million biomass gasifiers have been installed in India till 2016 (MNRE and IPNG Statistics Report, 2017).

3.1.4 Electric Stove

Electric stove is a compact and emission free clean energy product (Jain et al. 2015). It helps in avoiding the inconvenience caused with the procurement of Liquefied Petroleum Gas (LPG) for those living in urban slums, unofficial dwellings without legal status, since they do not possess necessary documentation to get subsidised LPG connection (ibid). An electric stove is a portable top stove that depends on electricity to power the appliance. Heat generated from the hotplate is made of a high performance, tubular element with a round cross section. Example of such product includes induction-based cooking. Induction stove operates on the principle of electromagnetic induction. On supply of electricity, the induction coil within the stove generates a magnetic field causing circular current to be rapidly created in the base of the cookware resulting in the generation of heat, which then directly transferred to the food being cooked. Analysis by Technavio in 2016 forecast that the induction cooktop market in India will grow at a Cumulative Average Growth Rate (CAGR) of 6.83 percent during the period 2016-2020.

3.1.5 Piped Natural Gas

Piped Natural Gas (PNG) is another clean energy product available for domestic, commercial and industrial consumption. It is an eco-friendly, pollution free, economical and safer fuel. With uninterrupted supply, there is no problem of storing the gas in cylinders. As per Bhagyanagar Gas Limited (BGL), a joint venture of Gas Authority of India Limited (GAIL) and Hindustan Petroleum Corporation Limited (HPCL), "PNG is one of the cleanest burning fuels which produces carbon dioxide and water vapour, thus helping in improving the quality of air". The technology is new, recently formulated and is in the process of implementation for the households in metropolitan cities of India.

3.1.6 Liquefied Petroleum Gas (LPG)

Liquefied or Liquid Petroleum Gas (LPG), is simply a propane or butane gas. It is a combination of flammable mixture of hydrocarbon gases. It is used as fuel for heating, cooking equipment and transportation. It is used as an aerosol propellant and as refrigerant. It replaces the chlorofluorocarbons in an effort to reduce damage to ozone layer.

According to Ministry of Petroleum and Natural Gas (MPNG), India has 252.1 million LPG connections as of Jan 2019. There is wide discrepancy in LPG use for cooking among states. According to a report by Petroleum Planning and Analysis Cell (PPAC) in 2019 the LPG coverage across the different states varied. Goa has the highest number with 139 percent. Telangana, Puducherry, Kerala and Mizoram are the other states with higher than 100 percent coverage. The southern states put together have a coverage of 99.7 percent while western states have 81.9 percent. Most north-eastern states have less than 80 percent coverage while the eastern states have the lowest coverage of 74.6 percent. The worst state among the LPG coverage are Jharkhand with 65.4 percent, Bihar with 67 percent and Odisha with 66.9 percent (PPAC, 2019).

3.1.7 Solar Based Lighting System

As per the rural electrification policy, a village is electrified if at least 10 percent of its households have been electrified by the central grid and minimum power provided is 6 to 8 hours per day (MoP, 2017). As per Central Electricity Authority (CEA) it was found that only 16 percent of the electrified rural households receive the entire 6 hours of electricity supply during the evening hours between 5 PM to 11 PM (CEA, 2017). With unreliable availability of electricity, people in rural areas use inefficient kerosene for lighting purpose (Dutt, 1994) which leads to many diseases. Use of kerosene and its byproducts also contribute to climate altering black carbon emissions (Jacobson, et al. 2013). As rural households purchase kerosene in large quantities, government also provide kerosene at subsidised rate regardless of the fuel causing adverse effect on the health and environment (ibid). For electrification of any village it has to be connected to the central grid, but it comes with some disadvantages. Use of centralised electrification system requires a high capital investment. It is less reliable, and results in fluctuation of voltage. Further, it leads to high transmission and distribution losses, results in environmental consequences and also poses a number of political, administrative, and technical challenges (World Bank, 2010).

These are not compelling benchmarks in the context of providing reliable electricity to all. Most of the rural areas with access to grid connected electricity face the issues related to reliability, availability and quality of power supplied (ibid). Electricity Distribution Companies (DISCOMs) understand rural households as non-revenue earners, due to issues of lower consumption, theft and distribution companies own inability to install meters and collect electricity charges effectively. Hence, they provide power to rural households on a rationed basis, so as to provide maximum power to urban households and industries (ibid). This reveals that there is a gap in rural energy supply which could be addressed through solar based lighting systems.

Solar based lighting system converts solar energy to produce electricity. This electricity is used to produce light. Example of such systems include solar home lighting system, solar lantern, etc. These systems consist of a Light Emitting Diode (LED), solar panel, battery, charge controller and an inverter. The light operates on electricity generated from solar photovoltaic (PV) panel and the energy is stored in a battery. The solar based lighting systems consist of both on-grid and off-grid systems. On-grid systems are connected to the grid, whereas the off-grid decentralised system are not connected to the grid.

Off-grid decentralised solar based lighting system are clean energy systems which are economically efficient, need oriented and equitable (Cabraal et al. 2005). "Off-grid solar based lighting system is an appropriate, scalable and viable solution for providing power to un-electrified, power deficient hamlets and villages (ibid). These systems are cheaper, reliable, require less time for installation, eliminate inefficiency when it is related to long distance transmission as the electricity is generated in proximity to the load and they have an improved cost-benefit ratio" (ibid). It can facilitate improvements in basic quality of life, productivity at the household and village level (ibid). These alternative solutions will allow local energy generation. It helps to overcome the demand for grid-based electricity and lessen reliance on costly traditional fuels (ibid). About 2.4 million solar lantern, lamps and 1.5 million solar home lights have been installed in India till Dec 2017 (MNRE, 2017).

3.1.8 Solar Based Irrigation System

"Sustainable agriculture is the central to achieve sustainable development goals from poverty alleviation to food security to livelihood security" (UN, 2015). Most of the future growth in agriculture is likely to come from intensification, in which irrigation plays an important role. For irrigation, we require energy which is fulfilled using a pump set run by diesel.

"India has about 21 million irrigation pumps, of which more than 9 million pumps run on diesel and another 12 million run on electricity" (Narale et al. 2013). Electricity consumption by irrigation pumps alone, consumes 15 percent of the India's total electricity consumption (ibid). These irrigation pumps are less efficient. Undertaking a grid connected system is also too expensive as the rural households are located in a faraway distance. Even if the fuel is available, it is difficult to transport to remote rural areas, because of poor physical infrastructure. Though government heavily subsidises agricultural grid connections but in rural areas there is intermittent, fraught with voltage fluctuations, with waiting time for an initial connection being too long (Banerjee et al. 2014).

To meet these challenges, solar based irrigation systems like solar operated pumps is an attractive option and is an alternative solution to those powered by grid electricity and diesel. It provides a better sustainable alternative option to fulfil irrigation requirement for agriculture purpose. Transportation of these systems is easy and convenient. It can be transported in pieces and again reassembled on the site. It requires low maintenance, less labour, no fuel cost and pumps water when needed. Solar based irrigation system converts solar energy to produce electricity. This electricity is used to pump water. "Solar based irrigation system is commercially viable irrigation technology, which has low operational and maintenance cost" (Yu et al. 2011). So far, 0.14 million solar pumps have been installed, including 0.31 million during 2016-17, 2017-18 and 2018-19 (PIB, 2017).

"Clean energy sources are the most outstanding alternative and the only solution to the growing depletion of fossil fuel reserves, greenhouse gas emissions, environmental concerns, geopolitical, military conflicts, and the continual fuel price fluctuations" (Tiwari and Mishra, 2011). They are sustainable and have a high degree of efficiency with respect to other technology options available for cooking, lighting, etc.

Energy is required at every level, starting from household to organisation level, from cooking to manufacturing to marketing of a product or service. As a result, the demand of energy is growing. Hence there is a need to look on the demand perspective for clean energy products. Thus, the next section focuses on demand for clean energy products in rural areas.

3.2 Demand for Clean Energy Products

According to a joint report by NITI Aayog and IEEJ in 2017, India's energy and electricity demand is likely to grow.

"It will grow at CAGR of 3.7 percent to 4.5 percent and 5.4 percent to 5.7 percent respectively till 2047, the pressure on natural resources to fuel the demand would only rise in the future. With a share of 18 percent in the world population, India consumes only 6 percent of the world's primary energy. This is evident from the low per capita energy consumption of India (521 kgoe in 2014) which is one-third of the world's average. Moreover, India houses nearly 304 million people without access to electricity (25 percent of the global population without access to electricity) and 800 million people without access to clean cooking fuels (30 percent of the global population without access to clean cooking fuels). India certainly aims to reduce its energy poverty in a sustainable manner keeping in mind the energy independence and the impact of these objectives on economic growth".

"Clean energy can become a critical factor for India's sustainable development agenda" (UN, 2015). Over the last few years Indian government has launched various schemes and supportive policies to encourage building up clean energy capacity and focus on clean energy generation in the country. The clean energy sector received a major lift after 2015, when the government decided to set a target to achieve a total capacity of 175GW from clean energy sources (excluding large hydro projects) by the year 2022. Out of 175GW, 100GW is from solar, 60GW is from hydro, 10GW from biomass and 5GW from small hydro (MNRE, 2017). Recently in 2019, India has again set to revise its target to achieve 227GW from clean energy sources. Out of 227GW, 113GW is from solar, 66GW is from wind, 10GW is from biomass, 5GW is from small hydro, 31GW is from floating solar, offshore wind and 2GW from others.

India has the largest potential for generation of energy from clean energy sources. The total clean energy power generation installed capacity in our country stands at 114.32GW, which is 33.23 percent of the total installed capacity of 344GW (CEA and IRENA, 2018). Installed clean energy power generation capacity has increased steadily over the years, posting a CAGR of 9.29 percent from 2008-2018 (ibid). India added a record of 11788MW of clean energy capacity during the year 2017-18. Power generation from clean energy sources (excluding the large hydro) in India reached 93.21 Billion Units (BU) in 2018 and India became the fourth largest installed capacity of wind power and the third largest installed capacity of Concentrated Solar Power (CSP) (IBEF, 2018).

With the target of achieving 175GW by 2022, the demand for electricity generation from clean energy has been increasing year by year. The clean energy generation in India was 81.88 BU in 2016-17 which has increased from 65.78 BU in 2015-16. This marked a 24.47 percent growth from 2015-16. Share of wind in total clean energy electricity generation has increased from 50.21 percent in 2015-16 to 56.19 percent in 2016-17. In the same period, share of solar has increased from 11.32 percent to 16.49 percent, with biomass, small hydro and waste to energy accounting for 17.28 percent, 9.68 percent and 0.37 percent respectively (Shaktifoundation, 2017). Table 2.2 highlights the electricity generation from clean energy (in BU) with share in total clean energy electricity from 2014-15 to 2016-17.

Table 3.2: Electricity Generation from Clean Energy (in BU) with Share in Total Clean Energy Electricity from 2014-15 to 2016-17.

Table 3.2: Electricity Generation from Clean Energy (in BU) with Share in Total Clean Energy Electricity from 2014-15 to 2016-17

Year	Wind		Solar		Biomass		Small Hydro		Waste-to-Energy		Total	% Growth
	BU	%	BU	%	BU	%	BU	%	BU	%	BU	
2014-15	33.77	54.65	4.60	7.44	14.95	24.19	8.06	13.04	0.41	0.67	61.79	-
2015-16	33.03	50.21	7.45	11.32	16.68	25.36	8.35	12.70	0.27	0.41	65.78	6.47
2016-17	46.00	56.19	13.50	16.49	14.15	17.28	7.92	9.68	0.30	0.37	81.88	24.47

Source: Compiled from CEA reports, 2017

During 2015-16 and 2016-17 the share of electricity generation from clean energy has improved from 5.61 percent to 6.59 percent of the total generation.

The significant point is the growth in generation from clean energy which achieved a quantum jump of 24.47 percent in 2016-17 compared to the previous year. In contrast, the growth in generation from conventional sources declined from 5.64 percent in 2015-16 to 4.72 percent in 2016-17 (CEA, 2017). Table 3.3 gives the generation from unclean and clean energy sources from 2014 to 2017.

Table 3.3: Generation from Unclean and Clean Energy Sources

Year	Total Gener ation (BU)	Conven tional Sources (BU)	Grow th in Conv entio nal (%)	Clea n Sour ces (BU)	Growt h in Clean Energ y (%)	Conventi onal share in total %	Clea n Ener gy shar e in total %
2014-15	1110.45	1048.67	-	61.78	-	94.44	-
2015-16	1173.65	1107.82	5.64	65.78	6.47	94.39	5.61
2016-17	1242.01	1160.14	4.72	81.88	24.47	93.41	6.59

Source: Compiled from CEA reports and Ministry of Power website, 2017

According to a report recently published by the Ministry of Power, Government of India, for the first time in 2016-17, clean energy capacity addition stood at 11.3GW which exceeded that of conventional energy, which stood at 10.3GW (MoP, 2017).

The demand for solar based lighting systems has gone up in recent years. Solar based lighting systems such as solar lanterns and Solar Home lighting System (SHS) have experienced an impressive growth between 2010 and 2017. Stood at 60 percent CAGR the products are notably the most significant technologies in this sector in 2017-18 in terms of market development, technological and business model innovation. In 2017-18 alone, an estimated 25.8 million off-grid decentralised solar based lighting systems were sold (REN21, 2018) and about 130 million off-grid solar based lighting systems were sold cumulatively by the end of 2017-18 (ibid), providing electricity to about 360 million people worldwide. Off-grid based solar lighting systems accounts for about 87 percent of the market (ibid).

In India, the cumulative achievement of off-grid solar based lighting systems under government programmes accounted to 762MW till July 2018. Of this, 104MW of capacity of off-grid solar PV systems was added in 2017-18 (CLEAN, 2018). The estimated sales of off-grid solar based lighting systems in India stands at 6.7 million units in the year 2017-18 (ibid). Maximum number of off-grid solar based lighting systems have been installed in Madhya Pradesh, followed by Rajasthan, Uttar Pradesh and Tamil Nadu (MNRE, 2017). About 57 lakhs solar based lighting systems have been installed by the end of Oct 2018 (MNRE, 2018). In Odisha about 90 thousand solar lanterns and solar operated lamps and 5 thousand solar home lighting systems have been installed till Dec 2017 (MNRE, 2017).

For increasing the demand for adoption of solar based lighting system, the MNRE provides Central Financial Assistance (CFA) to implementing agencies for deployment of solar based lighting system, solar street lights, solar pumps, solar power packs and other solar applications to meet the electricity and lighting needs of the consumers in the rural areas (MNRE, 2017). State Nodal Agencies (SNA) in the state are the primary implementing agency through which CFA of 30 percent is provided and for special category states and north-east states the CFA is 90 percent (ibid). Recently, the Ministry of New and Renewable Energy (MNRE) in 2019 has announced new benchmark cost for solar based lighting systems.

For off-grid decentralised solar powered system with a battery backup of 6 hours, the new benchmark cost up to 10kW is Rs 94/W and for a capacity above 10kW up to 25kW the new benchmark cost is Rs 84/W. Further, with a battery backup of 3 hours the new benchmark cost for general category states is Rs 66/W whereas for north eastern and hilly states, island and union territories the new benchmark cost up to 10kW with a battery backup of 6 hours is Rs 103/W. For capacity above 10kW and up to 25kW, the new benchmark cost is Rs 92/W. For solar based study lights the new benchmark cost is Rs 160/W compared to Rs 250/W for general category states. For the north eastern and hilly states, island and union territories the new benchmark cost is Rs 176/W compared to Rs 275/W in previous year.

For solar based irrigation systems, India has targeted to install 17.50 lakh standalone solar operated pumps for irrigation purpose (MNRE, 2017). Farmers will replace their diesel-powered pumps with standalone solar pumps which ranges from 0.5 hp to 10 hp (ibid). In the year 2014, the MNRE provided CFA of 30 percent of the benchmark cost of the pump. Further 40 percent capital subsidy from MNRE was also available with 20 percent beneficiary contribution, and the remaining amount was extended as loan, implemented through National Bank for Agriculture and Rural Development (NABARD). But in 2017, MNRE closed NABARD credit linked subsidy scheme and lay modified subsidy rates. The subsidy rates were 30 percent for pumps under 1 hp, 25 percent for 1 to 3 hp, and 20 percent for pumps 3 to 5 hp. In 2018-19 a new scheme was launched, called Kisan Urja Suraksha Evan Utthan Mahaabhiyan (KUSUM). It focuses on installing 2.75 million solar pumps of which 1.75 million will be off-grid solar operated water pumping system where the grid has not reached and another 1 million will be under grid connected. Under this scheme about 1.4 lakh crore financial assistance will be provided for installing 1 million grid connected solar based irrigation systems. A subsidised rate of 60 percent will be equally shared by the centre and state government, 30 percent financing would be done by bank and another 10 percent will be borne by the farmer for installing off-grid solar based irrigation system.

For increasing the demand for adoption of solar based irrigation systems, recently MNRE in 2019 announced new benchmark cost for standalone solar operated pumps for agriculture. For both direct current/alternative current (DC/AC) surface, DC/AC submersible, AC submersible, DC submersible, AC surface, DC surface, etc. for special category states the benchmark cost ranges from Rs 51,000/hp to Rs 1,19,000/hp and for north eastern and hilly states, island and union territories the new benchmark cost ranges from Rs 56,100/hp to Rs 1,30,900/hp. About 1.96 lakhs solar based irrigation systems have been installed by the end of October 2018 in India. Majority of the solar operated water pumping system has been installed in Rajasthan, Chattisgarh and Andhra Pradesh.

The demand for clean energy products needs to be accompanied with various factors which would help in diffusion of such products. Hence, the next section focuses on identifying such factors which affects diffusion of clean energy products.

3.2.1 Factors affecting Diffusion of Clean Energy Products

According to Oxford Dictionary, diffusion means "spread out over a large area". The concept of diffusion was first introduced by Tarde, as an "imitation" which is called "adoption". Adoption is the "decision to make full use of the product as the best course of action available". The concept of diffusion was further advanced by Rogers.

According to Rogers, "diffusion is the process by which an innovation is communicated through certain channels over time among the members of a social system". It can be simplified as, diffusion takes place through certain channels, may be through mass media or through interpersonal levels, over the time facilitated by some people. Diffusion is a special type of communication in which the messages (any new idea or thought) are transmitted to the population. Diffusion consists of several elements. The elements are innovation, communication channel, time and social system.

When any new idea or a thought is conceptualised, it is called an invention. When this idea or thought is put into a physical entity or is embedded into a product it is termed as innovation. Innovation is also viewed as an approach for better solutions that meet new requirements, unarticulated needs, or existing market needs. Innovation is also referred as the commercial applications of new technology, new material and new methods. When any innovative product is communicated into a social system, for commercialization, then it is also termed as diffusion.

Achieving universal access to modern energy is enshrined in U.N. Sustainable Development Goals because of its effect on human development. The world has already felt that the use of unclean energy is leading to global warming, formation of acid rain and depletion of ozone layer. As a result, the focus is now shifting for adopting clean energy in fight against the climate change. For achieving the same, there is a need to find the factors which affect the diffusion of clean energy products. Hence, this section focuses on identifying the different factors which affect the diffusion of clean energy products.

Solar based lighting systems are an ideal, cost effective technology available for lighting requirements (Schweizer-Ries, 2008). These systems are commercially affordable technology but are incompatible with personal priorities and compatibility (Berger, 2001).

Berger (2001) found that for diffusion of solar based lighting systems an appropriate marketing activity that increases familiarity, creating awareness by undertaking consumer education programs and using marketing materials for informing about processes through installation and service (ibid) needs to be undertaken.

Vaghela (1993) undertook a case study on adoption of solar products in the state of Gujarat in India and found that consumers are price sensitive. People who adopt such products are educated, have high income and high degree of awareness level. It was also found that family and friends become a strong influencing factor in buying decision, since word-of-mouth is a pertinent medium of communication. They play the role of opinion leaders and are important in making decision. Other factors identified from consumer perspective for adoption of clean energy products are size of the product, cost of the product, awareness on the product, availability of the product, availability of incentive, provision of after sales service and number of service centre present in the region.

Peter et al. (2002) studied on diffusion of solar operated products in developing countries and found that product characteristics, context (environmental, organisational and personal characteristics), demonstration sites, supplier characteristics, knowledge and familiarity affect the diffusion to take place. Product characteristics deal with attributes proposed by Rogers (1995) relative advantage, compatibility, complexity, trialability and observability, which has been discussed earlier. Further emphasising on the context, it deals with environmental characteristic, organisational characteristic and personal characteristics. Environmental characteristic includes stage of economic development, political stability, trade regulations and exchange rate of the region, where as organisational characteristics deal with individual characteristics, organisation internal characteristics, organisation external characteristics and personal characteristics. Internal characteristics are related to leaders' attitude towards change and external characteristics was related to system openness. Here system openness "is the degree to which members of a system are linked to other individuals who are external to the system" (Rogers, 1995). Internal characteristics of organisation is related to centralisation, complexity, formalisation, interconnectedness, organisational slack and size of the organisation. "Demonstration sites is also needed in different parts of the nation for creating awareness so as to enlighten the public on the benefits of using clean energy products" (Adurodija et al. 1998). In continuation to the study proposed by Peter at al. (2002) further Lehmann et al. (1974) and Katsikeas et al. (1993) supplemented it and gave other factors. Factors included reputation of the supplier, terms in financing, experience with supplier, reliability of the product, service support, training offered by the supplier, product quality, quick product delivery, competitive price, effective communication and availability of product parts also affects the diffusion to take place. Knowledge here deals with the awareness, how-to and principles knowledge. It is a chain process. Awareness leads to innovation required for solving a problem, further it leads to the process of information seeking, to know-how knowledge and finally to functioning of the innovation (Rogers, 1995). The cognitive state resulting from experience is familiarity (Peter at al. 2002). Familiarity comes through the degree of close acquaintance, a level of comfort, through exposure, experience and an attachment towards an innovation (ibid).

Gross et al. (2003) studied on the diffusion of solar photovoltaic (PV) technology in Ghana and found that price of the product and availability plays a bigger role in the diffusion of the product. Brown (1981) focused that until government, entrepreneurial or non-profit organisation makes the innovation available at or near the location of the potential adopter, consumer will not have the option to adopt in the first place. Thus, availability plays an important role in the diffusion of clean energy products.

Reddy and Painuly (2004) studied on the barriers for solar technology diffusion in the areas of Pune and Mumbai of India. Their study involved households, industrial firms and commercial establishments and it was found that awareness level, knowledge level of the adopters, cost of the product, consumer perceptions about the quality of the product, usefulness of the product and advice from friends were the major factors affecting the diffusion to take place. Apart from the above factors, it was also highlighted that availability of skilled workers and technical specifications of the product do also affect the diffusion to take place.

Gebreegziabher (2012); Heltberg (2004) and Leach (1992); Caird et al. (2008); Akinboro et al. (2012) investigated the energy efficiency and clean energy technologies and found that adoption of these technology depends upon financial aspects of the product. Factors such as cost, practical issues regarding installation and level of general knowledge, awareness level, income level and education level do also affect the diffusion to take place.

Mavuri (2011) undertook a study on solar water heater in the city of Visakhapatnam in India and found that education level and those having high income were aware of the product. Moreover, it was also found that family and friends were having a strong role in the diffusion of the product. Other factors included size, cost, awareness, availability and serviceability do also affect the diffusion to take place.

Samantha (2011) undertook a case study on enabling frameworks addressing solar water heater technology in Tunisia and found that public awareness, acceptance by the people, quality assurance, private sector participation and policy support do also affect the diffusion to take place.

Ijeoma (2012) found that repairing of broken parts of a clean energy product and time lag between breakdown and repair were responsible for diffusion to take place.

Lay et al. (2013) undertook a study in Kenya on diffusion of solar operated lights and found that education level, income level of the household, the household expenditure, ownership of the dwelling, rural setting of the household, the prevalence of Solar Home Systems (SHS) in the area and availability of technical assistance for installation and service were the major factors that helped the diffusion to take place. Further, it was also found that apart from the quality aspect of the product, hours of operation of the light do also affect the diffusion to take place.

Bairiganjan and Sanyal (2013) studied on solar home lighting system and found that there were cases of technology deployment being unsuccessful when the companies did not focus on establishing a proper supply chain to provide maintenance and quick replacement parts of the product. Establishing of proper supply chain and with timely replacement of the defective parts were responsible for the diffusion to take place.

Martinot et al. (2000) and Weinthal (2015) added that for diffusion of any clean energy product, manufacturers need to develop market generation policies, establish effective equipment standardisation and adopt different certifications associated with it in order to safeguard quality of service and affordability. These would help in diffusion of clean energy products.

3.2.2 Categorisation of Factors Affecting Diffusion of Clean Energy Products

Different factors were identified which affected diffusion of clean energy products in particular. In table 3.4 an attempt has been made to categorise the factors under four major categories. It includes finance, capacity building, technology and infrastructure related.

Table 3.4: Categorisation of Factors Affecting Diffusion of Clean Energy Products

Major Factor	Sub-Factors	Proponents
Finance related	• Income level • Affordability • Cost of the product • Availability of incentive • Terms of financing • Financial aspects of the product • Household expenditure	Vaghela (1993) Martinot et al. (2000) Heltberg (2004) Reddy and Painuly (2004) Gross et al. (2003) Caird et al. (2008) Mavuri (2011) Akinboro et al. (2012) Lay et al. (2013) Weinthal (2015)

Major Factor	Sub-Factors	Proponents
Capacity building related	• Education level • Awareness level • Undertaking education programs • Advice from friends • Knowledge level • Offering of training by supplier	Vaghela (1993) Reddy and Painuly (2004) Schweizer-Ries (2008) Mavuri (2011) Samantha (2011) Akinboro et al. (2012) Lay et al. (2013)
Technology related	• Size of the product • Product characteristics (relative advantage, compatibility, complexity, trialability and observability) • Consumer perception about the quality of the product • Features of the product • Reliability of the product • Usefulness of the product • Practical issues regarding installation • Quality assurance • Technical assistance for installation and service • Hours of operation of the product	Vaghela (1993) Rogers (1995) Peter et al. (2002) Reddy and Painuly (2004) Mavuri (2011) Samantha (2011) Akinboro et al. (2012) Lay et al. (2013)
Infrastructure related	• Provision of service and number of service centres • Demonstration sites • Supplier characteristics • Reputation of the supplier and experience • Quick delivery • Acceptance by people • Participation, policy support and political stability • Ownership of the dwelling • Rural setting of the household • Proper supply chain • Repairing of broken parts • Time lag between product breakdown and repair • Availability of the product • Availability and quick replacement of the defective parts of the product • Market generation policies • Equipment standardisation and certifications on safeguard on quality and good service	Vaghela (1993) Rogers (1995) Peter et al. (2002) Martinot et al. (2000) Gross et al. (2003) Mavuri (2011) Samantha (2011) Ijeoma (2012) Lay et al. (2013) Bairiganjan et al. (2013) Weinthal (2015)

As per Tawney et al. (2013) for diffusion of clean energy products, "access to finance is very essential". Banks and other financing institutions need to act as an intermediary between the rural consumers and clean energy product manufacturers. The manufactures of clean energy products need to work with collaboration with different financing institutions, particularly the branches of the banks based at rural areas, for providing loans to the consumers (ibid). Finance plays an important role in the diffusion of the clean energy product. The identified factors were categorised under finance related. As per the report by UNDP in 2015, "the capacity development of individuals, organisations, etc. is necessary for development towards transformation". Capacity building focuses on the effort to teach and make someone learn and do something better (ibid). Here the focus is on providing education and training. It deals with developmental approach leading to transformation (ibid). Transformation through education and training will help in empowering the individuals, organisations, etc. (ibid). For example, providing training and conducting workshops help in enhancing the skills and enabling the trainees to train others in using clean energy products. It is termed as capacity building (ibid). Capacity building plays an important role in the diffusion of the clean energy product. The identified factors were categorised under capacity building related.

Technology is all pervasive. From the literature, an understanding has been made that technology is more confined to technical aspects, methods of production, design, specifications, etc. Technology plays an important role in the diffusion of the clean energy product. The identified factors were categorised under technology related.

Kabiru (2016) has focused that infrastructure is necessary for diffusion take place. Infrastructure "means the facilities which are needed for growth of the nation" (ibid). It consists of economic infrastructure and social infrastructure. "Economic infrastructure helps in growth of economic development of the country" (ibid). It deals with the basic physical infrastructure such as availability of electricity, proper transportation and energy while the social infrastructure deals with the basic infrastructure required for people's development such as availability of health centres, educational institutions, housing facility, etc. Functionally, infrastructure speaks about production of goods and services, distribution channels, and from social perspective it focuses on healthcare and educational services available (ibid). Infrastructure plays an important role in the diffusion of the clean energy product. The identified factors were categorised under infrastructure related.

After categorisation of factors which affects diffusion of clean energy products, there is a need to understand the various activities within and around an organisation which together create a product or service (Porter, 1985). Value chain is a tool to comprehensively identify the activities undertaken by a firm from raw material sourcing to product or service delivery to the customer. Fig 3.1 represents the value chain analysis.

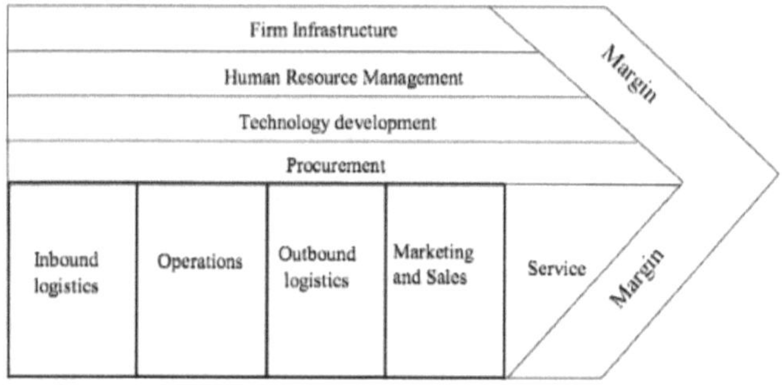

Fig 3.1: Value Chain Analysis

Value chain consists of primary activities and support activities. Primary activities are those which are basically required for the manufacturing of physical product or in rendering of service, delivering and marketing of the product to the buyer and providing after sales service. These include inbound logistics (deals with receiving, storing, distributing, stock, transport, etc.), operations (deals with machining, packaging, assembly, testing, etc.), outbound logistics (deals with warehousing, material handling, distribution, etc.), marketing and sales (deals with awareness about the product, advertising, selling, etc.) and service (deals with service delivery, product installation, repair, training and availability of spares). These activities are also linked to support activities.

Support activities are those activities which help in providing inputs or infrastructure that allow the primary activities to take place. It includes activities such as procurement, which deals with acquiring various inputs such as the raw materials, services, tools and machinery, etc. It extends across the entire value chain as it supports each activity and each activity uses purchased inputs of some kind. Technology development surrounds the activities which are involved in designing the product and manufacturing it. In fact, every activity a firm undertakes involves the technology or technologies which may be tedious or sophisticated. It basically involves a variety of activities, some are performed outside the research and development department. It also includes the human resource management which deals with recruiting, managing, training, developing and rewarding of personnel. Each activity undertakes human resource as they are the assets of the organisation. They cut cross the entire value chain. Finally, the firm infrastructure includes the activities such as the general management, accounting, planning, finance, legal, quality control, information management and all other activities are required for the entire value chain to operate.

In the context of economically poorer region especially in the rural areas, lack of availability of reliable technology at an affordable price hinders the pace of socio-economic development. For last three decades, like technology and market-based approach to development has been all pervasive, hence there is a need to relook marketing of products in the rural areas. Hence, the subsequent sections focus on the rural market perspectives.

3.3 Characteristics of Rural Consumer

In India, with more than 800 million people reside in rural areas. It has caught the attention of businesses for their products and services. With continuous increase in purchasing power of rural people and saturation in urban markets, the focus of attention of companies has moved to rural areas. Inspite of the importance of the rural markets for the growth of the economy and wellbeing of people, our understanding of the complexities and nuances of rural marketing are still evolving. Understanding the consumer's needs and their characteristics is an important aspect of rural marketing. Consumers in rural areas have become a significant market for consumer durable and non-durable products and services like agri-inputs and outputs, food, construction, electrical, electronics, automobiles, finance, insurance, health, education etc.

Rural consumers having unique social and cultural backgrounds which have put the manufacturers into a challenging situation for developing strategies to reach out to them and sale their products. There is a need to understand the characteristics of rural consumers, but let us first understand the evolution of rural market.

Rural markets are as old as India itself. However, the traditional rural market gave way to modern market with the onset of liberalisation, privatisation and globalisation of Indian economy in the last decade of 20th century. Rural marketing evolved in four phases: Self-sufficient village economy (<1960), Green revolution era (1960-1990), Liberalised era (1990-2000) and ICT era (>2000). After independence and till 1960, rural India behaved like a self-sufficient village economy. The producers and consumers were in close proximity. Barring a few products from faraway places with the onset of green revolution in 1960, the rural market saw the predominance of agri- inputs and output service. It continued till 1990, the beginning of liberalisation, privatisation and globalisation. It opened rural market to goods and services from faraway places. The needs and wants of rural consumers got influenced with global consumers. However, with ICT diffusion in 2000, the process of integration into global economy got accelerated. Table 3.5 indicates the stages of evolution of rural marketing.

Table 3.5: Evolution of Rural Marketing

Phases of Rural Marketing Evolution	Breakthrough	Key Characteristics
Phase-I: Self-sufficient village economy (<1960)	Agricultural marketing	**Product**: Rural produced and consumed, urban produced and rural consumed and rural produced and urban consumed. Consumer durable: traditional, simple, need oriented. **Price**: Low price, Barter system and Mortgage **Place**: Haats, Melas **Promotion**: Direct visualisation, Word of mouth, Persuasion.
Phase-II: Green revolution era (1960-1990)	Green revolution and White revolution	**Product**: Agri-inputs like: high yield seeds, Tools, Tractors, Fertilisers, Pesticides, Pumps, Sprinklers, Cattle feed, Milk production and Packing, etc. **Price**: Subsidised rate **Place**: PDS, Melas, Producers cooperatives **Promotion**: Rally, Government supported exhibitions
Phase-III: Liberalised era (1990-2000)	Industrial growth	**Product**: All industrial products, households consumables and durables, service sector was strengthen **Price**: Low, High **Place**: Mandi, Wholesalers, Retailers, Kirana stores **Promotion**: Print media
Phase-IV: ICT era (>2000)	Technology, Communication network and infrastructure development	**Product**: New product developed, high end consumer durable and FMCG products **Price**: High/Low, Discounted rate, Subsidised rate **Place**: Haats, Melas, SHG, Wholesalers, Retailers **Promotion**: E-commerce platform, Advertisements in TV, Internet, EMI schemes, Extended warranty.

With the birth of "Green revolution and White revolution", agri-inputs were given to the rural consumers in subsidised rate. Government supported exhibitions, rallies, etc. were conducted as a promotional effort for diffusion of the products. Products were sold in melas, Public Distribution System (PDS) stores, etc. During the liberalisation era, more importance was given to industrial sector. Industrial products were manufactured, focusing on household's consumables and durables. Local governance and reforms got a boost. Promotion of products were taken up through print media and others. Products were sold through wholesalers, retailers, small kirana stores, etc.

From the onset of 21st century, ICT played a major role. With the introduction of World Wide Web (www), it opened the market. Infrastructure availability in the form of electricity and motorable road enabled marketing of high-end products through e-commerce platforms. Attractive financial schemes, bank subsidy and welfare schemes of government added steam to the existing momentum. In the second decade of 21st century many companies increased investment in rural areas. However, the problem of affordability, information asymmetry and distribution of products or services, remain a challenge for many rural markets.

Earlier, rural consumers used to live in isolation and were shy to meet the community at large and were economically backward. As urbanisation and industrialisation is growing rapidly in our country they are transforming. With changing of time and economic condition improving, they are becoming more literate and value driven (Kashyap, 2012). They are being influenced by urban consumption pattern. With increase in their income, desire to satisfy their needs and wants have led to demand for various products. They are no more satisfied with cheaper and poor-quality products. They demand on quality and aesthetic products at low price. The rural youths are becoming the "key drivers for expenditure", in the form of mobile phones, bikes, personal care products, etc. for improving their quality of life (Kashyap, 2012). According to Mohanty (2013), "rural youths have emerged as opinion leaders in influencing the brand and making product decisions in a market that was swayed by village elders for centuries". They have become growth drivers of new products coming into the market. They demand products with high quality and low price. Here the manufacturers need to find out not the right consumer for their products but rather the right products for their consumers. In simple words, it is the marketing mix which helps to understand what product or service could be offered and how to plan for a successful product offering. The feature of marketing mix is consumer, who is the focal point for any marketing activity. According to McCarthy (1964), "Marketing mix is a pack of four sets of variables, namely product variable, price variable, promotion variable and place variable". These elements of marketing mix have been described in the next section.

3.4 Marketing of Products and Services in Rural Areas

Marketing of products and services in the rural areas takes place by the marketing mix elements. Basically, there are four elements of marketing mix. It includes Product, Price, Place and Promotion. Each of these elements has been discussed below.

Product is the key element in the market. It fulfils the needs and wants of the target consumer. According to Ferrell (2005), "product is the essential part of the marketing mix strategy where the retailers can tender unique attributes that differentiates their product from their competitors". According to Borden (1984), "product is identified by its design, properties, quality, brand name and sizes". A rural consumer seeks the product features, quality, service associated with it and its cost, before going for purchasing any product.

In the rural context there are different classification of products. According to Kashyap (2012) classification of rural products has been carried out on the basis of convenience, shopping, specialty and agri-inputs products. Products of convenience include FMCG products, cosmetics, toiletries, etc. Shopping products include clothing's, furniture, appliances, etc. Specialty products cover machineries (wheeler, tractors etc.), electronics items (camera, mobile phone etc.), etc. Agri-inputs include fertilisers, pesticides, organic material, etc. This classification lacks robust logic. Kashyap (2012) further refined the classification of rural products by dividing into FMCG, durables, services and agricultural goods given in table 3.6.

Table 3.6: General Classification of Rural Products

Rural Products	Products
FMCG	Toiletries, Cosmetics, Foods and beverages, Footwear
Durables	Home appliances, Automobiles, Watches, Furniture
Services	Healthcare, Banking and insurance, Education, Telecommunication, ICT
Agricultural goods	Tangible goods used in farm activities, products of allied sector, agri-input markets

Source: Kashyap, 2012

Here the durable products are those which do not wear out quickly, one that yields utility over time rather than being completely consumed in one use. Highly durable goods such as refrigerators, cars usually continue to be useful for three or more years of use (OSullivan and Sheffrin, 2003). In the above classification, the durables like home appliances, automobiles do overlap with the agricultural goods. Further, agricultural goods like tractors, power tillers, sprinklers, etc. are also the durables products which are useful for more than three or more years. Examples of some of the consumer durable products include automobiles, books, consumer electronics, furniture, tools appliances etc. (ibid). One can classify the products used in rural areas based on their needs, place of availability and paying capacity. Every individual requires right product or services for satisfying his/her need. Such needs can be classified from Maslow's need hierarchy. In rural context it will include appropriate products and services for satisfying physiological, safety and security, social, esteem and self-actualisation needs given in table 3.7.

Table 3.7: Classification of Products used in Rural Areas

Need	Products
• Physiological needs	Food products, Clothing products, Household and Furnishing products, Medicines
• Safety needs	Insurance products, Retirement and Investment products
• Belonging needs	Personal and Grooming products, Jewellery products

Need	Products
• Esteem needs	Luxury products, Expensive products
• Self-Actualisation needs	Hobbies, Travel and Educational products
Paying Capacity	
• High paying capacity	Branded products, Luxury products, Innovative products
• Low paying capacity	Unbranded products, Low priced products
Place	
• Rural centric products	Agricultural tools, Carpentry products, Organic products

Rural products are broadly classified under three categories such as need, place and paying capacity. Need is required for any organism necessary for a safe, stable and healthy life (e.g. food, water, shelter). Here need is required at every level such as in agriculture, health and hygiene, education, communication, etc. Paying capacity is another category where the products can be classified as branded products, luxury products and innovative products for a high paying capacity group. Similarly, for a low paying capacity group they generally prefer unbranded products which are low priced. Place basically consist of where the rural centric products are available, which are majorly used in rural areas, like agricultural tools, carpentry products, organic products, etc.

From a basket of different products or services that has the potential to satisfy certain need, a costumer will buy that product which meets the criteria of availability, affordability, durability, timeliness and image. For example, LED lights manufactured in China and sold in India is easily accepted in the market due to their low cost, easy availability and easy to use. It can increase its value if it is durable, can go for multiple usage, easy to install and maintain and provide immediate benefits. Rural consumers also respond to those products that corresponds to their religious faith, social norms and assist in their traditional occupations and life style.

Based on value proposition any marketer before offering any product needs to think on the product offerings in the form of basic product, expected product, augmented product and potential product (Kashyap, 2012). Any product with minimum features to perform its function as perceived by producer is a basic product. A product with all the features that are required to satisfy the reasonable expectations of the consumer (in contrast to as perceived by the manufacturer) is called expected product. An augmented product includes features beyond the immediate reasonably expected use of the consumer. A potential product has features beyond the potential (imaginable) expectations of the consumers. For example, solar based lighting system for a rural consumer which offers lighting need only, is termed as basic product. If the solar based lighting system has the provision for different modes of lighting with a rechargeable battery along with timely maintenance and having a warranty period, then it is termed as expected product. If the same solar based lighting system comes with a mobile charger and with a slot for operating a portable fan or a television, then it will be treated as an augmented product. Use of solar based lighting system for unexpected use, such as for income generation activity is an example of a potential product. Hence, any type of product, that a rural consumer thinks to buy, depends on factors such as cost-benefit of the product, level of awareness towards the product, purchasing power of the consumer, verification or demonstration of the product, availability of customised product, utility of the product, ease of installation, maintainability, aesthetic, attitude towards the product, opinion leader's roles and the consumer's own view. A manufacturer while selling a product in the rural areas, should consider all the above factors mentioned.

Price is "the settlement for any product or service charged" (Kotler et al. 2008). It is also defined as the "total value that a consumer exchange for the benefits of having or using the product or service" (ibid).

In the present context, rural consumers are price-sensitive, and it affects their buying decision. They prefer to buy those products which are not only low in price but also have discounts, credit and phased payment facility (Kashyap, 2012). Some of the pricing strategy which can be offered are product bundling strategy and product-sharing strategy.

Goods are produced to be sold to the consumers. It is required to be made available to the consumers at a place so that they can conveniently purchase. According to Berghman (2006), "A place is used for effective distribution of the firm's products among the channels of marketing like the wholesalers or retailers". "A place should provide all information about the consumer, competition, promotion action, and marketing task" (ibid). Emphasis should be, on how to deliver the product at right time and at right place and which channel to be used for achieving it. For distribution of products in the rural areas focus should be on the places/ actors/ platforms of various rural centric models. These distribution models include haats, village malls, petrol pumps, NGO, rural innovation centre, SHGs, and cooperatives. A brief description is given for different rural centric models.

Haats: It is one of the oldest of all the marketing channels in rural India. It offers a wide range of products or services to rural consumers clustered around its location (Adite, 1996). It sells fresh vegetables, fruits, garments, groceries, agricultural inputs and equipment, consumer expendables and many spurious products (Sathyanarayana and Ganesh, 2008). Its frequency of occurrence is 1 to 4 times weekly depending on the availability, occasions, demand, etc. It acts as a base for supporting and providing a platform for trading purpose in rural areas.

Village Mall: Recently the state Government of Andhra Pradesh introduced the concept of "Village Mall", under the caption called 'Chandranna Village Mall' which is being supported under Prime Minister Mudra Scheme. These malls sale basic items, household items, beauty items and other domestic items. Under this approach, the ration shops of the state are converted into semi-super markets which offers different products, apart from the state government sponsored subsidised items. Here, the discounts offered by the companies to the village malls will be distributed in the ratio of 60:40 to the consumers and dealers respectively. Products being offered in discount rate will benefit the poorer sections of the society. This unique Public-Private-Partnership (PPP) model is an attempt to modernise Public Distribution System (PDS) in the state through an innovative model having dual benefits of PDS and modern retail.

Petrol Pumps: They act as a platform for distribution of products in the rural areas. Bharat Petroleum is the second largest oil marketing company in India, with over more than 6000 retail outlets spread across the country. "InandOut Convenience Store" is a unique concept launched in 2001, where different types of FMCG products are sold. It is set up mainly in the urban markets and at other sub-urban areas strategically located retail outlet sites where there are high consumer footfalls. Today more than 240 "InandOut" stores are present across the country. These stores promote various schemes and offers which are being offered by the petroleum company.

Associated Distribution: This type of distribution can help in diffusion of clean energy products in the rural areas. Here two companies can come together and jointly distribute the products into the rural areas. They share the distribution cost. Here the small company tie up with the prime company that already has a presence in the rural area for distribution of the products through its distribution network, with the regulation that the small company will not dispense the same product which the prime company is selling. For example, considering the sale of solar operated irrigation system a partnership can be created with the bank or the cooperative to enable the consumers to take loan for the product and pay it through instalments.

NGO: They play a significant role in diffusion of clean energy products in the rural areas. NGOs can facilitate both upward and downward communication from consumers to the manufacturers and manufacturers to the consumers. NGOs need to communicate information about their needs, wants, purchasing power, attitude, cultural characteristics, etc. of the consumers to the manufacturers and manufacturers need to consider NGOs as their channel partners. They can act as a point of sale for different products being manufactured. They act as a synergy between the manufacturers and the rural consumers.

Rural Innovation Centre: Recently Harsha Trust, an NGO working in the South Odisha, in tribal dominated area started "Rural Innovation Centre" in Bissamcuttack in Rayagada District of Odisha, India. This centre is supported by Axis Bank Foundation and has the most advanced soil testing lab and a cold storage plant working on solar energy. The primary objective of this centre is to reach out to tribal and poor communities and development practitioners. These kind of centres can act as a demonstration hub for using of clean energy products in rural areas. Here, the rural innovation centre can also become a point of sale and be a channel partner for several FMCG companies.

SHG: Here "SHG do play an important role in distribution of products in the rural areas" (Ramanathan, 1993). When products are distributed through the members of an SHG, it affects their purchase decision. SHGs can have a direct contact with the manufacturers for procurement of the products, as a result they can become channel partners. Manufacturers can make SHG as their rural stockiest and proponents of products and service providers. They can act as product pushers rather than channel members. For distribution of products by SHG members they need to develop a relationship with local retailers in order to enhance the supply chain network. SHG members can act as rural agent and get commission to push the product onto the doorsteps of the rural consumers.

Cooperative Society: It can play an important role in distribution of products in the rural areas. Here, the products from the producer or the manufacturer comes directly to the cooperative. A regional sales officer or the area manager needs to coordinate with representative of the cooperative to ensure that products are sold, and cash is collected in a timely manner. The cooperative can bear the freight charges from the manufacturer's plant to the cooperative warehouse. Cooperative employees those involved in the distribution process need to be provided with training on different aspects like storing, handling, maintaining of stock, book keeping, etc. of the products.

Other possible distribution channel partners can be a post office, which can act as a point of sale, promotion and distribution of the product. A photocopy shop, electrical shop and local tiffin stall can be a channel partner for distribution of products in the rural areas. Distribution channels in the rural areas can be classified on the basis of ownership of producer (haat, village mall, petrol pump), ownership of consumer (cooperative society) and ownership of both producer and consumer (rural innovation centre and SHG). The ownership refers to the organisation that is involved in different stages of value chain till the delivery of product and services to its end consumers. Another way of classification can be on the basis of direct layers and indirect layers. Direct layer does not involve any intermediary between the consumer and manufacturer (zero layer). Examples are haat, cooperative, SHG and village mall. Indirect layer occurs when there are middlemen or intermediaries within the distribution channel (multi-layer). Example a petrol pump.

Promotion is defined as the "sales promotion, advertising, personal selling, public relations and direct marketing" (Kotler et al. 2008). As per Lovelock et al. (2004), "promotion is the decision of relating the product to the target market segment and how to convince the customers to buy it". "Creating awareness and inducing trial", of a product are the key objectives of promotion (Kalotra, 2013). Activities that are linked to promotion are advertising, sales promotions, personal selling and publicity.

Advertising is an element of promotion mix, where the information is dispersed to the consumers by non-personal means through paid media where the source is the sponsoring organisation. Sales promotion deals with consumer promotion by using certain tools such as giving of product samples, coupons, prizes, cash refund, etc. and adopting trade promotion such as giving allowances, merchandise allowances, co-operative advertising, advertising and display allowances, dealer sales contests and sales-force promotion such as providing bonuses, going for contests, sales rallies, etc. Personal selling is another element of promotion, where the information is dispersed by non-personal means to the customers through face-to-face interactions and demonstration of the product. Publicity is another element of promotion, where it deals with mass communication. It uses certain tools such as giving public speeches, interviews, individuals or organisations offering donations, going for inauguration of huge events by celebrities, etc., that attract the mass media to produce the news about them. These activities influence consumer's way of thinking, affect their emotions and experiences as their purchase decision (ibid). Manufacturers need to design the communication process in such a way that it should provide a stable message about the products or services and persuade the prospective consumers to buy and use the products.

In the rural context, consumers purchase the product by seeing, touching and feeling. Rural consumers like to purchase the product from known and fixed retailers who maintain close family relations with them. "Advertising through television and radio are most effective in the rural setting" (Kalotra, 2013). For promotion of products in rural areas, there is a need to have an effective promotional effort, involving visual and pictorial illustrations in local or regional language. Some of the strategies which can be adopted for creating awareness and promotion about a product or service is by conducting door-to-door campaign, cycle rally, participating in rural melas, trade fairs, exhibitions, conducting road shows, street plays, campaigning through auto-rickshaws by using loud speakers for communication purpose, conducting puppet shows, showing documentary films, etc. All these strategies act as an important communication tool for getting the rural consumers aware about the products or services. After understanding the marketing mix variables, fig 3.2 gives the marketing mix diffusion factors framework.

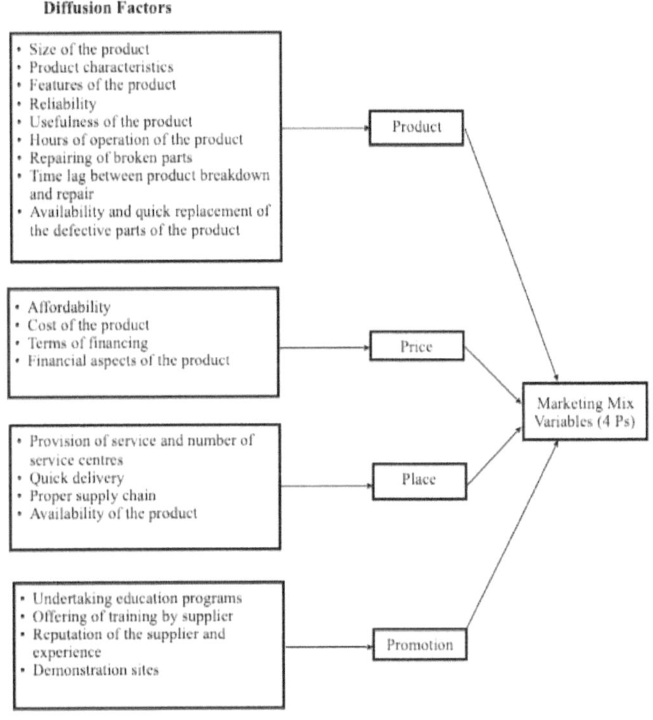

Fig 3.2: Marketing Mix - Diffusion Factors Framework

From table 3.4 which provides different factors affecting diffusion of clean energy products, an attempt has been made to place these factors under different marketing mix elements and the framework was termed as marketing mix-diffusion factors framework, represented in fig 2.2. Product refers to the goods and services offered to the consumers. It not only focuses on the physical product itself, but it also deals with the size, characteristics, features of the product, reliability, how useful the product is in satisfying the requirement of the consumer, hours of operating, and various services associated with the product like repairing, replacement, etc. Price refers to the amount a manufacturer charges for the product or service. It focuses on the cost of the product, financing aspects available for purchasing of the product, such as EMI, subsidy, etc.

Affordability is defined as the product needs to be cheap so that a consumer can afford to buy it or pay for it. It means the manufacturer needs to provide the product at an affordable price. Place focuses on the distribution channel. It is used to get the product reach to its consumers. It deals with the number of service centres present in the region, providing quick service delivery of the product and ensuring availability of the product when demanded by the consumers. Promotion refers to the advertising and making the consumers aware about the product available in the market. Promotional activities deal with undertaking education programs and sensitising the consumers to understand about the product, usability of the product, and need of the product. It also focuses on the provision of providing training to the supplier/manufacturer of the product to adopt which kind of communication channel to reach its consumers. Reputation of the supplier/ manufacturer and experience do influence the consumer to adopt the product. Quick service delivery by a particular supplier/manufacturer brings more consumers which help in adoption of the product. Demonstration of product in different sites, is a promotional strategy where a product is demonstrated to a probable consumer in hope of purchasing the product. It helps the consumers see the product in action and grasp its value and potential. It thus helps in serving the purpose of instilling a sense of ownership of the product to the probable consumers.

3.5 Difficulty of Diffusion of Clean Energy Products in Rural Areas

"More than a billion people in the world do not have access to electricity and are suffering both socially and economically and live without access to electricity" (Mathur et al. 2015). Inaccessibility to electricity leads to problem such as low level of education, income, and poor health (ibid). According to Murali et al. (2015) "there are millions of households in India which are either un-electrified or receives unreliable electricity for which they depend on the use of kerosene, wood and other conventional sources of energy". To overcome this problem the use of clean energy products can play a significant role.

But despite of advancement in technology and financial options available for several clean energy products, there has been a difficulty in diffusion of clean energy products in rural areas. Hence, there is a need to identify those factors which creates barrier in the diffusion process (Luthra et al. 2015). These factors have been identified from various literatures whose study has focused on Indian rural context.

Painuly (2001) identified different factors which act as a barrier for diffusion of clean energy products in rural areas from world perspectives. Lack of information and awareness, restricted access to technology which focuses on either the technology not available or available at high cost, missing market infrastructure that focuses on under-developed supply channels, poor logistics, inconvenient product location, requirement of high investment, subsidies available to use of conventional energy, taxes on purchase of clean energy products, economically not viable, high payback period, high cost of capital, lack of access to credit to rural consumers, lack of financing institutions to support Renewable Energy Technologies (RETs), lack of instruments, lack of institutions mechanisms to disseminate information, lack of R&D culture, lack of private sector participation, lack of standard and codes and certification, lack of skilled personnel and training facilities in the rural area, lack of entrepreneurs and lack of consumer acceptance of clean energy product are the factors which creates difficulty in diffusion of clean energy products in rural areas.

Yaqoot et al. (2016) found some factors which negatively affect the adoption and diffusion process. Factors like poor design of the product, lack of availability of skilled man power, high upfront cost, policies favouring conventional energy through subsidies and other incentives, inadequate incentives to promote the diffusion of clean energy products, poor purchasing power, lack of access to credit availability, lack of awareness of the technology, product and service associated, lack of consistent policies and regulations, lack of coordination between various stakeholders that is poor monitoring and evaluation, un-satisfied perceived needs and non-integration of technology with the current societal norms and preference for going for traditional energy sources and showing resistance to adopt new technologies are the major factors which creates difficulty in diffusion of clean energy products in rural areas.

Luthra et al. (2015) identified some factors which act as a barrier for diffusion of clean energy products in rural areas from Indian perspectives. Factors like high initial capital cost, lack of financing mechanism, lack of subsidy availability, like rebates, tax exemption, low interest loans, lack of awareness for technology adoption, lack of paying capacity, price of the product, less efficiency, lack of availability of spare parts and trained people, lack of R&D work, lack of experience, cultural belief and faith and lack of political commitment to adopt clean energy products creates difficulty in diffusion of clean energy products in rural areas.

Holtorf et al. (2015) identified different factors which act as a barrier for diffusion of clean energy products in rural areas. Factors like lack of technical knowledge, lack of private sector involvement, lack of involvement of local stakeholders, lack of capital, lack of high capital cost, lack of credit, no income generation, poor maintenance, poor installation, limited product availability, insufficient logistic infrastructure, donor dependency and no link to existing social structures and values are the factors which creates difficulty in diffusion of clean energy products in rural areas.

Kweka (2011) identified high initial cost of the system, lack of establishment of dealer network and secure after sales service, limited awareness, low purchasing power of rural consumer, limited technical knowledge on installation, operation and maintenance, difficult in accessing the finance were the major factors responsible for difficulty in diffusion of clean energy products in rural areas.

Martinot et al. (2000) identified different factors which act as a barrier for diffusion of clean energy products in rural areas. Initial purchase price, lack of information on product, cost and benefits, lack of information on product quality and performance and poor quality of the product were the major factors responsible for difficulty in diffusion of clean energy products in rural areas.

Urmee et al. (2016) identified different factors which act as a barrier for diffusion of clean energy products in rural areas. Lack of availability of the product and spares parts, no information on government subsidy, lack of technical knowledge, lack of involvement of local communities in program implementation, non-availability of credit, lack of financing and improper management were the major factors responsible for difficulty in diffusion of clean energy products in rural areas. For diffusion of clean energy products in rural areas the identified difficulties need to be addressed. Moving on to the next chapter, it focuses on entrepreneurial eco-system.

CHAPTER FOUR

ENTREPRENEURIAL ECO-SYSTEM

By 2020, the most trending word or the concept has been "Entrepreneurship", across the world. India as a country has been talking and seeing many entrepreneurs coming up in the recent years. Even the government, private bodies, education system and many institutions are taking various initiatives and steps to promote Entrepreneurs and Entrepreneurship. There are schemes, subsidies, funds, grants, etc by both State and Central Government to promote entrepreneurship. In 2021 and 2022, India has generated the highest number of Unicorns. India has emerged as a great competitor to nations like the US and China, in terms of creating businesses and entrepreneurs. Infact, other countries and corporates are now preferring India as their business target market.

Interestingly, other than Government and Private bodies, even Educational Institutes have taken leadership roles in promoting startups and in the field of clean energy and sustainability. Educational roles have created a separate Centres for Entrepreneurship to prioritize or focus on aspiring entrepreneurs and ideas. They take the responsibility to identify the entrepreneurs, mentor them, help them with setting up an organization, prepare project reports, explore markets and even connect to the investors and banks. Similar are the centres set up by the State and Central Governments, to ensure that an entrepreneur is given the right platform to grow their idea to a full fledged business, sustain it and also scale it up.

This chapter has three sections. First section focuses on organisations and startups working on clean energy products. Second section emphasises on the benefits and the last section focuses on cultural aspects of entrepreneurship.

4.1 Organizations and Startups working on Clean Energy Products

Many states in India such as Rajasthan, Gujarat, Andhra Pradesh, Karnataka, Telangana and Tamil Nadu have already started giving emphasis on renewable energy by creating various renewable energy hubs. And organizations such as Solar Energy Corporation of India (SECI), The Indian Renewable Energy Development Agency (IREDA), National Institute of Wind Energy (NIWE) and National Institute of Solar Energy (NISE) are well known for their interventions, innovations and programmes on clean energy products and services. Big corporates such as

Tata Power, Suzlon Energy, Renew Power, are making huge impacts through their investment on Renewable Energy field. Tata Power has three business segments on renewable energy i.e. manufacturing of solar cells and modules, engineering, procurement and construction (EPC) for solar power projects and other solar products. It helps to provide solutions to various sectors such as banking, education, telecom, healthcare, and many more. It not just operates in urban areas but also caters the rural population. Around 30% of Tata Power's total capacity is currently from clean energy, and it aims to contribute 80% by 2030. Suzlon Power is well known for designing, developing and manufacturing Wind Turbine Generators (WTG). Though it has its presence in 18 countries, it has installed its largest wind energy capacity unit in India. ReNew Power Ventures also is into the generation of non-conventional energy through solar and wind power. In India, it sells its power to large industries and also to state electricity boards. Looking at the future scope, the company has plans to double the capacity of its running plants and upcoming projects.

There are many startups that have received funding for their innovative ideas, and ofcourse the market demand. Ace Green Recycling is a battery recycling startup, which claims to have developed clean and efficient lead-acid battery recycling technology. It seems the battery that the start up has developed operates at room temperature, contains zero air emissions, and wastes and reduces heavy metal emissions, resulting in significantly lower environmental damage. The startup has raised a fund of $10 Million. CleanMax Enviro Energy Solutions provides renewable electricity. It has already raised a fund of more than $188 Million and is planning to scale its industrial renewable energy space, not just in India, but also in the Middle East and SouthEast Asia.

As we understand, pollution has been a key issue in many metros, Tier 1 and even a few Tier 2 cities, not just in India but also in other countries. India has been promoting many startups that are working to address the pollution issue through its innovative products and services. Startups like Devic Earth have developed air pollution controlling equipment for large scale industries that helps in improving the air quality of that area. Chakr Innovation is a startup that has developed an emission control device that can check the pollution level and capture emissions of harmful particulate matter. It has raised more than $3.6 Million. There are many startups that caters to micro and small scale industries as well. Startups like Freyr Energy help in setting up the solar system in the small industries and even residential and commercial complexes. It has raised $4.6 Million, and is looking to working towards mass market adoption of solar energy. Inficold is a startup that provides cold storage solutions to small industries through its modular cold storages.

India has been promoting alternative fuels for a couple of years, and intends to not be dependent on petrol or diesel which the country has to import to suffice the need. Hence, startups that develop automobiles with alternative fuel or batteries help the economy as a whole. Startup like Gegadyne Energy has developed an eco-friendly alternatives to lithium-ion batteries, with quick charging feature. It has raised more than $5 Million. GPS Renewables is a startup working to solve the problem of organic waste management. It plans to substitute fossil fuel with bioenergy. It has raised $23 Million. Green joules has developed renewable biofuels from agri residue and wastes from agro processing industries. It has raised fund of $330 Million. It is also working to develop high energy density liquid and gaseous biofuels.

Not just in India, there are startups across the globe which have seen huge growth in the renewable energy sector.

4.2 Benefits that India Has

In 2021, In terms of renewable energy capacity and wind power, India ranks 4th globally and in terms of solar power capacity, India ranks 5th globally. India ranks 3rd on the EY Renewable Energy Country Attractive Index 2021.

Prime Minister of India, Shri Narendra Modi, at an event had announced that the capacity of renewable energy in India has increased by a huge percentage of 250% in between the Year 2014 and 2021. This shows the country's priority in terms of the importance of Clean Energy Products, and the policies to promote businesses in these fields. The Central Government of India has allocated Rs. 19500 crore which translates to US$ 2.57 billion, in its Union Budget for 2022-12, for a Production Linked Incentive (PLI) scheme to boost the manufacturing of high-efficiency solar modules. In 2021, it also launched a global initiative to accelerate and promote innovation in the field of clean energy for all the countries, named as Mission Innovation CleanTech Exchange.

In the last two decades i.e. 2000 to 2021, India has received an Foreign Direct Investment of approximately US$ 11.21 billion in the renewable sector. Such huge investment helps to promote the clean energy sector in the country.

The Central Electricity Authority estimates that the demand for energy will also increase drastically by 2030. The major demand is expected to come from the real estate sector as well as the transportation sector.

India is developing its policies and strategies that promotes the development of clean energy products, services and technologies. Proper regulatory policies, advanced systems and technologies, tax relaxation, emphasis on research and development, and looking for the investment opportunities in renewable energy sector are few key areas where India has been prioritizing for a few years now.

4.3 Entrepreneurship as a Culture

In India, if there are thousands of new entrepreneurs and hundreds of unicorns within just 12 months, then it cannot be an overnight result. It has to be the result of efforts made by various stakeholders in the past few years. The stakeholders could be Central Government, State Government, Investors, Banks, Educational Institutes, Consultants and Entrepreneurs themselves. If any one of the stakeholders is not willing to coorperate in the process, then the progress might not have happened the way it has taken place, especially in Indian context.

4.4 Conclusion

Not just in India, but the entire world is now thinking of ideas those are environment friendly and sustainable. Like mentioned before, many educational institutes are having centre for entrepreneurship and a separate centre for renewable energy to give their focus on innovating, designing and developing clean energy products. And those centres work in close coordination to create meaningful entrepreneurs who not just create businesses but also create products that saves the environment, that saves the world. The next chapter focuses on the role of education in enhancing quality of life of rural people.

CHAPTER FIVE

ROLE OF EDUCATION IN ENHANCING QOL OF RURAL PEOPLE

One of the crucial elements of regional development that the federal government should support is rural education. Putting policies into place, it makes it easier for other performers to perform the new roles they have taken on. Local government should give more authority and serve as the focal point for local development as a result of decentralisation. Both local communities and the federal government should be effectively connected to local governments. They should be expected to carry out certain tasks that the central government has previously handled, including specific legal and regulatory obligations as well as the provision of services like extension. Additionally, they should be given more responsibilities as a result of the growing emphasis on globalisation and its associated changes as well as the increased demand and diversity of economic activity. As a result, they can involve providing local communities with guidance, particularly during the initial stages, assisting in the development of their capacities, fostering relationships between community organisations and the organised commercial sector, setting up monitoring mechanisms, etc.

5.1 India's Rural Schooling Environment

Developing and strengthening local institutional capacities, improving rural infrastructure and related services, a supportive policy framework (such as policies to promote financial intermediaries in the rural areas), developing agriculture as well as rural industries and other off-farm activities, providing education, skill training, health and other essential services, and most importantly, developing agriculture are all necessary for the realisation of effective rural development. Policies, development plans, and even programmes and initiatives created at the highest levels of government, occasionally with donor funding, may not always take into account the needs and capacities of local populations. As a result, these initiatives failed to address the unique issues faced by various communities and social groupings. The word "education" has a Latin etymology, "Educatio," and throughout the development of human civilisation, we have been able to associate it with several meanings. The noun "EDUCO - education" and the verb "educo - Educator" both contain the Latin prefix "Educatio," which has the meanings "out of," "to elevate," and "to increase." In the function that education plays in the development of human values essential to shaping, nurturing, and developing the spirit, both meanings are linked. If we examine the meanings, purposes, and investment in education over the entire growth of human society, both strategies of reforming education emphasise capacity constant attribute. Education serves to transition a person out of their natural state and into their cultural state. In a civilised society, education play a crucial role. First, it helps shape and develop a person's unique characteristics. A comprehensive understanding of education's place in society is necessary because a nation's economic growth is correlated with its citizenry's degree of education.

5.2 Rural Areas' Socio-Demographic Patterns and Processes

In today's fast-paced, information-rich world, managers' ability to motivate employees to provide desired performance in rural areas is their most crucial task. As regions grow, managers must continue to exercise their expertise and grace in the art of motivating employees. Currently, rural communities need to develop their social surroundings. The ability to compete is crucial in rural areas. Indian reality is made up of a mix of towns and villages with a known population distribution: Compared to metropolitan areas, rural areas make up 64.61 percent of the population. The village continues to be the primary supporter of rural life today. The nation's poverty weight as well as the burden of elderly people and dependent children fall disproportionately on the countryside, which is an astonishing but terrible power. For this additional national demographic burden, many more villages take it upon themselves to care for two thirds of the elders and children without any assistance from the state.

5.3 The Development of Rural Development Strategies

In the past, governments in poor nations and international donors conducted their development initiatives using a "domain approach." This strategy had drawbacks, and it has been determined that domain investments by themselves would not be sufficient for rural development. While this strategy may have the potential to enhance the delivery of public services, it is evident that it frequently encourages the decentralisation of domain-specific Ministries and Departments and obstructs real decentralisation. Additionally, cross-domain problems are not addressed. Therefore, it has been realised that domain investments and programmes must be coupled with decentralised integrated development efforts in order to obtain the anticipated benefits of the decentralisation efforts.

Community development depends on the emergence of a sense of community. Respecting the "felt needs" of the various local communities is also important. These are the needs as seen and experienced by the neighbourhood, which may differ from those "needs" that have been determined by "outsiders". People should be consulted about their preferences and informed about them. Effective decentralisation might bring about institutional change that is more suited to this kind of regional strategy. Local government institutions and community organisations in particular could form a cooperative partnership to take on the responsibility of creating a local "vision" and strategy, as well as designing, planning, allocating resources, implementing, and monitoring/evaluating development activities that would better meet local needs. They would "jointly" take the reins of their development projects, cultivate a "feeling of shared ownership," and act as "managers." Top-down approaches to development in the past had a negative impact on rural development, which is now "supply-driven" in many nations.

Top-level government officials formulate policies, development strategies, and even programmes and initiatives. The quality of governance at different levels, the effective devolution of responsibility and authority to local levels, the transformation of public institutions and change in attitude, the availability of resources including financial, human, physical, and natural resources, the strength of local organisations and local governments, the participation of locals, and a number of other factors all affect how successful decentralisation is. Decentralization has its limitations, which local governments and communities must effectively handle. For instance, many of the limitations that existed before to decentralisation may take some time to resolve. The goals of education and educational processes are so complex today that only a concentrated effort from many institutions, embodied in what some have dubbed "the city of education," by "redistribution" of education by a number of factors, could result in actions with satisfactory results. It would therefore appear to be beneficial to restructure the social functions of various departments in relation to educational requirements.

Today's schools are not longer closed institutions isolated within strict regulatory frameworks; rather, they are an outward, interconnected component of the contemporary social system. Currently, science and education both have a role in how people develop as individuals and as a society. Teacher intervention is crucial to students' growth inside the educational system. School, students' formal education, and instructors' labour are all seen as influencing factors in how young people develop in conformity with societal expectations.

5.4 An Educated Life and Being

People who have received a quality education have a better grasp of their surroundings and are therefore less sensitive to outside influences. Education is necessary for accurate information interpretation since it advances knowledge. An educated individual is more aware of their rights, the purposes of others in society, and their own. It will raise emotional quotient. The rural person(s) can improve; they can become more understanding, caring, and self-sufficient; they can learn to love themselves before others while remaining selfless. So, this is how education improves quality of life. It has the power to alter one's outlook on life.

In India, education in the rural areas is crucial for a number of additional social, economic, cultural, and political reasons in addition to helping to end poverty and illiteracy. Urban and rural education have a critical role in the development of the national economy. A rural education system has the potential to increase the capacity and knowledge of the rural population, empowering them to make informed decisions about their farms and to innovate in the field of agriculture. Additionally, education exposes the public to knowledge and aids in avoiding information misunderstandings. Children attending school can grow more conscious of their environment. It would enable them to comprehend the laws, regulations, rights, obligations, and numerous other plans that are applicable to them.

5.5 Conclusion

Education is more important now than it has ever been. It is the new unit of account for the world economy. The more you have, the better off you and your family will be. It is crucial for success. "Man only develops into a man through education" (Kant). Next chapter covers the impact of consumer's education on eco-consumption.

CHAPTER SIX

EDUCATION AND ECO-CONSUMPTION

This chapter highlights on the concept of eco-consumption. It basically focuses on the impact of education on eco buying decision of the customer. Today's growing climatic glitches and health menaces has created a buzz in the society. These environmental threats created a nightmare for Government, researcher, NGO's, business and customers.

Very interestingly business impending with an elucidation to customer's problem introduced eco-products which further successful in developing the craze within the conscious mass which gave rise to a new-fangled notion of eco-consumerism. The present study focuses on effect of education on eco-consumption and enhances the relation between education and other demographic factors by the use of contingency table.

Environment is a burning issue in today's era. On one hand this technical era has gifted the human race with amazing range of products to make life easy and comfortable, on the other hand, unknowingly it has snatched the purity of nature which not only leads to climatic entanglement but also the cause of numerous diseases. Today is the high time to buzz the alarm. In order to create a green society, business very successfully inoculated the spark of eco-consciousness through the use of eco-product which further led to the growth of eco-consumption.

Eco- Consumption is analyzing the evolving sensation of the terms called "eco-chic: anamalgamation of lifestyle politics, spirituality, environmentalism, health and beauty" (Barendregt, B. and Jaffe, R., 2014). Eco-chic ties sustainable, ethical and elite consumption (ibid). Education is considered as one of the important determinant of eco-consumption so perception and awareness of consumer is analysed with respect to eco- consumption.

6.1 Literature Review

Table 6.1: Citation on Effect of Education on Eco-Consumption

S.No	Author, Year	Findings
1.	Boztepe, 2012	While green promotion affects green purchasing of elementary schools, green price and green product features affects for high school graduates purchases and green product features, environmental awareness and green promotion affects the purchasing for undergraduate and graduate customers. So it is found from overall study that education moderately affects green consumer purchase.
2.	Shahnaei, 2012	There is a positive impact of higher education level on green purchasing in Malaysia.
3.	Diamantolopous, Schlegelmilch, Sinkovics, Bohlen, 2003	A study in Britain there is a positive correlation between education, information and attitudes and behaviour.

4.	Tilikidouve Delistavrou, 2001	As per a survey in Greece more frequently pro-environmental non-purchasing behaviours are seen in educated mass.
5.	Afzaal Ali, 2012	Survey shows that eco-consumption is getting lower with education level, researcher argues bachelor respondents have more favorable attitude towards green purchase intention as compared to those respondents with higher education.
6.	Christopher Gan, 2008	Postgraduate Degree, positively impact the eco-consumption.
7.	Joonas Rokka, 2008	Persons with the highest education levels were found to have more favorable behavior towards all environmental aspects, but they are skeptical about the eco-claims made by firms.
8.	Zuraidah Ramly, 2012	Empirical exploration showed environmentally conscious behavior among educated Malaysian consumers.
9.	Khandoker Mahmudur Rahman, 2011	Research shows a positive correlation between "willingness to pay premium" and "education level" of customer.
10.	Jurate Banyte, 2010	The results support that more educated customers have a better eco sensitive.

6.2 Objective

The objectives of this study are as follows

To study the impact of education on eco-consumption.

To know the relation between various demographic factors with education.

To know the level of consumer awareness and perception of customers with respect to education.

6.2.1 Hypothesis Formation

H1: Association between Education and Product features of eco- friendly products.

H2: Association between Education and Pricing of eco-friendly products.

H3: Association between Education and Labeling of eco- friendly products.

H4: Association between Education and Packaging of eco- friendly products.

6.3 Methodology

Primary data is used for analysis of data. The sample was collected from about 200 respondents from Odisha whereas only 160 samples were found suitable for further analysis. It is the first hand data incurred through interview and observation conducted on people who use eco-product. Data analysis was carried out by taking contingency table and Chi-Square test. As, Odisha is our sampling location and population is large enough for survey so researcher had to consider some areas of Odisha by using stratified sampling technique and respondents by using simple random sampling technique.

6.4 Result and Discussions

This section of the chapter focuses on the descriptive analysis of the consumer data regarding demographic profile. The current analysis of the respondent's demographic dimensions provides a clear understanding of the customer background. Demographic outline covers the sample size of (n=160) consumers which includes gender, age, marital status educational qualification, income and occupation.

Survey shows that female are more conscious than male considering green FMCG product awareness, purchase and consumption. Hence, it was concluded that higher educated people mostly purchase and consume green FMCG products. It was also found that 35 percent of the respondents were private employees, 20 percent were housewifes and 20 percent were Government employees.

These are those occupational group who were mostly environmental conscious compared to other occupational groups. As 58 percent of respondents were married. It was found that married people were more conscious about green FMCG products in comparison with 42 percent of unmarried respondents. From the survey it was found that most of the respondents belong to the income group of between 75,001 to 1, 00,000.

Table 6.2: Survey on Education of Customer with Respect to Occupation

EDUCATION vs OCCUPATION								
Count of RESPONDENTS	OCCUPATION							
EDUCATION	Business	Government Employee	House Wife	Others	Private Employee	Students	Unemployed	Grand Total
Above PG	4	9	4	1	10	4	1	33
Post Graduate	4	11	7	0	13	6	1	42
Graduate	3	13	8	0	14	7	0	45
Intermediate	7	2	5	1	6	4	2	27
Matriculation	3	2	3	0	3	0	2	13

Current table shows the relation between Education and Occupation.

Interpretation: As per the survey above PG respondents who were mostly inclined towards eco-product were private employees and house wives. Survey also shows post graduates who believe in eco-consumption are private employees and housewifes. In case of graduates, occupation preference was basically both Government and private employees. In case of intermediate/diploma there are only 10 respondents who were private employees. From above interpretation it was found that most of the eco conscious customers were either private employees or housewife with post graduate or above post graduate and some of them were graduate working in Government sector.

Table 6.3: Survey on Education of Customer with Respect to Income

EDUCATION vs INCOME								
Count of RESPONDENTS	INCOME							
EDUCATION	Less than 15,000	15,001-30,000	30,001-45,000	45,001-60,000	60,001-75,000	75,001-1,00,000	Above 1,00,000	Grand Total
Above Post Graduation	0	2	4	6	7	8	6	33
Post Graduate	0	2	4	8	9	11	8	42
Graduate	1	3	5	9	8	10	9	45
Intermediate	5	7	6	5	4	0	0	27
Matriculation	6	5	2	0	0	0	0	13
Grand Total	12	19	21	28	28	29	23	160

Current table shows the relation between Education and Income.

Interpretation: From the above table it was found that higher education (Graduate, PG and above PG) with higher income (75,001- 1,00,000) are generally inclined towards eco-product.

Table 6.4: Survey on Consumer Perception on Green Products with respect to Education

Count of Respondents	Awareness		
EDUCATION	No	Yes	Grand Total
Above Post Graduate	4	29	33
Post Graduate	12	30	42
Graduate	12	33	45
Intermediate /Diploma	16	11	27
Matriculation	9	4	13
Grand Total	53	107	160

Current table shows the customer preference with respect to education of the respondents.

Interpretation: From the survey it was found that post graduate, above post graduate and graduate prefer green products compared to non-green products. It was found that consumer's perception among the highly educated people is positive about the environment.

Table 6.5: Survey on Consumer Awareness on Green Products with respect to Education

Count of Respondents	Awareness		
EDUCATION	No	Yes	Grand Total
Above Post Graduate	1	32	33
Post Graduate	2	40	42
Graduate	2	43	45
Intermediate /Diploma	16	11	27
Matriculation	8	5	13
Grand Total	29	131	160

This table gives idea about consumer's awareness with respect to education.

Interpretation: From the present study 61 are above post graduate, 72 are post graduates, 53 are graduates, 15 are intermediate/diploma and 3 are matric qualified and 2 are below 10th. They are aware of green FMCG products. Finding shows that educated customers are more conscious and aware about green FMCG products and its uses.

Table 6.6: Analysis of the Result

S.No	Hypothesis	Chi-square value	Remark
H1	Association between Education and Product features of eco- friendly products.	27.808 (0.033) *	Accepted
H2	Association between Education and Pricing of eco-friendly products.	31.745 (0.11)*	Accepted
H3	Association between Education and Labeling of eco- friendly products.	44.983 (0.000)**	Accepted
H4	Association between Education and Packaging of eco- friendly products.	41.646 (0.000)**	Accepted

*Significant at $p < 0.05$, ** Significant at $p < 0.01$, ***Insignificant at $P > 0.05$

6.5 Conclusion

Eco-consumption is becoming the buzz of the society. When the light is put on awareness and perception towards this green product it's really appealing. Even it is seen that educated people are more conscious about eco-consumption. But, when the attention is given towards eco-consumption habit of the customer is not so alluring. From the present study it was found that there is a significant relation between education, occupation, income and buying intension of customer towards eco-product. It is the high time to embellish the eco-culture and change to eco- behaviour by adopting green practices. Next chapter focuses on role of training and development for rural people.

CHAPTER SEVEN

ROLE OF TRAINING AND DEVELOPMENT FOR RURAL PEOPLE

This chapter focuses on the role of training and development in an NGO. Rural Development has always been a matter of concern in India. It is never a new theme. Non-Governmental Organizations (NGOs) play a vital role in rural development. NGOs conduct several developmental programmes to improve the condition of rural areas. The workers of NGOs work effectively towards rural development. The workers of NGOs are effective, dedicated and committed towards nature of service and have recognized number of roles which can affect rural development. NGO as a subject suffers from theoretical vacuum. Given proper weightage it can be a complex phenomenon comprising myriad activities. In broader perspective NGOs can prove to be more elastic and multi dimensional unit that can help in all round development of rural areas. It is essential for NGOs to undergo proper Training and Development activities so that the workers can alleviate poverty in the rural areas. Poverty amongst the rural areas can effectively be eradicated if the workers are properly trained who can contribute to the growth of rural areas. The workers can contribute to the growth of rural areas if they are trained with adequate skills to provide minimum service that can improve the quality of life of the poor.

There are various reasons to answer the question why is training important for the staff and workers of NGO sector. One of the main reasons is to ensure staff development and skills strengthening are the fact that the NGO sector has such a significant impact globally which impacts rural areas of Odisha. There are around 3315 NGOs in Odisha, but nevertheless they are very well trained or equipped with skills to develop the rural areas of the State.

In fact, the number of people anticipated to contribute to charities by 2030 is 2.5 billion, and 80% of the global populations believe that NGOs make it easy to be involved in positive social change. The scale of the sector is clear when you consider that "if NGOs were a country, they would have the 5th leading economy in the world". We cannot deny the fact when power comes it comes with huge responsibility, and the importance of staff development is thus unquestionable. This chapter has two sections. First section focuses on NGOs in Odisha and the second section is the conclusion.

7.1 NGOs in Odisha

Non-Government Organisations (NGOs) in Odisha play a major role in social development and welfare of the state people. The Odisha NGOs are joining in Social Growth and Charitable matters organized by Government and other self help groups.

Odisha has the third largest number of villages in India, next only to Uttar Pradesh and Madhya Pradesh. There is a need for growth of such villages with the objective of making them more viable village. It is a well known fact that Odisha NGOs are performing helpful programmes for social welfare matters, charitable purposes and support. They are always ready to come forward to work for the betterment and upliftment of the children, women development and help to the old age homes and people. NGOs are organizing various beneficiaries programmes from time to time related to Child Education, Child Welfare, Child Rights, Women Development, Women Empowerment, Employment, Animal Welfare etc. This is possible with the help of trained NGO workers perhaps they can reduce the number of sustainability amongst the villages. In the view of the high unemployment rate, it is alarming that some skills need to be deployed among the workers of NGO to make them capable to eradicate ignorance among the rural areas. Due to the lack of training and development skills the workers are unable to address the high unemployment situation in maximum part of Odisha. NGOs have become essential in development and nurturing of rural areas which are often neglected by government. Sustainability of NGOs is a huge dilemma as many have taken their hands back in providing them service and getting involved. NGO has been proactive in addressing unemployment and work creation in the rural areas of Odisha.

Non-Profit Organizations provides in the creation of local work opportunities that are currently given to the third party. NGOs also provides in the up skilling of Job seekers. So if we really want to bring a positive change in the rural areas the NGO workers should be properly trained through a systematic path as follows:

7.1.1 Identify the Training needs through Training need Assessment

At first we need to identify the gap areas where the training is required. A proper analysis should be done to find out these gaps. It can be done through questionnaires or focused group discussions etc. It will also answer to the question that whether training is actually needed or not. Based on the category of NGO we can decide the method of assessment.

7.1.2 Set the Objectives of Training

In the next stage once we get the needs identified, we need to form the objectives of training to attain these needs.

7.1.3 Finalize the contents or topics for the Training

In the next stage we need to finalize the contents of the training, its modules and process of imparting these training effectively. We should be first clear with the contents that we are going to make our workers learn in the training programme.

7.1.4 Preparation of Training Design

In this stage we need to prepare the roadmap for training, this is the most important stage out of all stages where we need to design the outline of training. The success of training depends on how much carefully we have designed the outline of the training and how we have set the goals of training. In this stage we need to determine the process or methodology of proving the training. There may be different methods for different modules or topics. Thus our training design should include:

- What subjects to be provided in the training
- What methods will be adopted for the contents
- What resources will be needed

7.1.5 Develop a module for the Training

In this stage modules will be prepared as per the gaps found out in the 1st stage of training. The module should include step by step procedure of every session that will be provided in the training. In other words it should have a session and its description of how to go ahead with the session smoothly. The basic reference materials and guiding materials should be included in this stage.

7.1.6 Oraganize the Training: In this stage the actual training sessions are organized and conducted as per our designed modules.

7.1.7 Evaluation of the Training: Assessment of training is most crucial step to find out whether the objectives of training are fulfilled or not. Thus, we should not forget to assess the training programme provided. We may have any type of assessments like mid-term evaluation if it's a long term training programme to judge whether it's going in the right direction and mend it if required. A participatory evaluation is always more helpful.

Knowledge is Power! Knowledge never gets unused; in fact it enhances and monitors a person towards long-term and sustainable development. An educated person is valued everywhere. With this objective, we should ensure that every NGO worker should be provided with the best skill development training keep in the mind the development of children, youths, women and key stakeholders for integrated and all round development.

Focus should be on following:

- Increased productivity and performance in any setting
- Skills development
- Training of Trainers
- Team development
- Replication of models
- Systems strengthening
- Training and Development (T&D)

The training provided should be pertinent to the needs of individual worker and their organizations with an importance on the hands-on application of participants' learning back in the work place. For example, if an NGO is providing charitable services to children, a moral training course may include local laws and customs governing the types of relationships aid workers may and may not have with those children. Other ethical training may be targeted more toward illustrating the correct procedures for accepting and receiving donations that are collected.

Another example, if the NGO delivers medical services to a remote, needy population, an all-purpose training session might cover the origins of the program. The goal here would be to provide workers with contextual material so that they can recognize and converse how the organizations are developed. In contrast, training for staff members who actually provide the medical services would likely be much more directed to specific procedures and protocols.

7.2 Conclusion

In a state like Odisha where three-fourth of its population is living in villages, the all round development of rural areas acquires a significant importance. Rural development has been an important topic for the government of Odisha right from the beginning. Rural development in Odisha is a very comprehensive and multidimensional process. In this case, NGOs a new form of non-profit organization can play a very significant role in people's participation through creating awareness, educating, motivating and enlightening the people for social transformation. They are instrumental in initiating, stimulating and accelerating the process of change in the tradition bound rural society. Studies have proved that NGOs are exceptionally made for the developmental purpose and as a catalyst of social change. NGOs are considered as good educators, as informers, as experimenter, as promoters, as consciousness producers and conscientizers as 'friend, philosopher, and guide' of the people in general and of the weak, poor, needy, demoralized and deprived sections of the society in particular. It is evident that NGO has made efforts to promote the economic well being of the poor people and yet they are not completely successful to a larger extent because they are not well trained to do so. Indeed, proper training is very important for them if we want sustainable development of Odisha. Moving on the next chapter it covers some marketing models for clean energy products in rural areas of Odisha.

CHAPTER EIGHT

MARKETING MODELS FOR CLEAN ENERGY PRODUCTS IN RURAL AREAS OF ODISHA

This chapter focuses on the different marketing models for clean energy products in the rural areas of India in general and Odisha in particular. A survey has been undertaken in some parts of South Odisha where there was prospects of marketing of solar lights. This chapter has two sections. First section focuses on different models and also suggest some strategies for marketing of clean energy products in the rural areas of India in general and Odisha in particular and the second section focuses on the survey and the implementation of Entrepreneurial-cum- SHG Model

model for easy adoption of clean energy products in rural areas.

8.1 Marketing of Clean Energy Products

The size of rural market for clean energy products is huge but the the companies generally target the rural region closest to its area of operation, a convenient and obvious choice for them by which people living in distant are deprived of it. Hence, an effective distribution model should be in place for last mile consumer (Solanki, 2005). The prices for all these clean energy products should be kept low or the same unless it is manufactured in large whether it is consumer electronic, FMCG or renewable energy product (Solanki, 2005). Direct marketing is an option, by having a store in a rural location such as electrical stores, mobile sales and service shops, cable TV DTH service shops, etc.

The crucial factors for a broader marketing of PV systems are: financial incentives, government led initiatives, reduction of investment costs, and increase in reliability, dissemination of information and environmental awareness. A persuaded individual can make quick adoption decision rather than a person with inadequate awareness and knowledge. There are different marketing and selling strategies which are being adopted for rural consumers depending upon the location. Factors that help in promoting the clean energy products business includes documentation, quality, process, design and innovation, production capability and, finally, cost effectiveness, etc.

Among the few which are required for marketing are, door to door selling of clean energy products, selling in haats, melas, etc. There are different models of distribution as well. Most effective is the Entrepreneurial-cum- SHG Model which is discussed in the later part of the chapter.

Here, the members are sensitized for using clean energy product for lighting purpose and other income generation activities. Explaining and demonstrating the use of clean energy product to the SHG members at the village level during their weekly meetings, preferably in evenings is a low cost distribution model which is needed to be adopted for PV penetration in the rural areas of India and Odisha.

Affordability, availability are the major concern for any rural consumer to think before purchasing any product. Having access to credit facility is a major issue for rural people to purchase any product. They need to spend less but they deserve a good quality product. Many households in rural areas neither have access to electricity, and more importantly, nor do they have access to credit. Why is access to credit important? When a reliable product say a solar light is introduced into the market its cost is naturally higher which in turn makes it not affordable to buy.

Affordable does not mean its cheap quality product but rather it should be able to generate repayments and help in income generation. Rural consumers should be provided with a low-interest credit which becomes a headache for both institutional and financing organisation. For example, if a household wants to purchase a solar home lighting system, then he finds it difficult to pay the full amount, now some of the organisations are giving these systems on credit and going for payments in a Equal Monthly Instalments (EMI) but it affects the organisation in terms of the running of the business the operational cost more precisely to say. Hence, a desirable system such as, jointly purchasing the product and giving it for rent, would be a good option.

There are different branding and advertising strategies for selling of products in rural areas, but for clean energy products the following strategies such as, word of mouth where the company people organise "tea party" at the home of satisfied customers, where people from around the village are invited to watch a demonstration of how the clean energy product is functioning. They do often create noise so that people come outside of their homes to see what is happening which further acts like a free publicity (SELCO Case Study). Other strategies such as banks themselves plays an important role in marketing the clean energy product at their own branch, when they identify a potential customer or lead who could afford and benefit from the system they provide loan to purchase it.

Another model is the demonstration model where the company installs a system in the house of a influential or wealthy person of the village for one-to-two month on trial. The program starts off with a tea party similar to one described above. At the end of the trial period technicians return and began to disconnect the system. The experience of living with the product along with the family and social pressures eventually induced most customers to take the loan and purchase the system (SELCO, Yale SoM, Case Study).

Product share pricing strategy is another strategy, where the rural consumers can share their clean energy products with other consumers. For example the use of clean energy operated drip irrigation system purchased by a farmer at Rs 25000 was shared with other farmers for irrigating their fields which could be near by. The system is given on rent with a specific amount, on per hour basis or per day basis. This business model can act as an income generation activity for the farmer and subsequently helping him to good quality of life. Clean energy sector is an emerging industry. Showcasing clean energy products, demonstrating in trade shows, exhibitions, melas, etc. are some of the powerful avenues for marketing the clean energy products. Participating in an expo attract good number of customers and subsequently helps in building a network chain of customers, if the product is of good quality. It helps in scaling up the production and fulfilling the target.

Clean energy products can be financed through micro-credit to rural people. Micro credit refers to purveyance of loans in small quantities. The term "micro" literally means "small", as per micro credit special cell of the Reserve Bank of India (RBI), the borrowing amounts up to the limit of Rs 25000 could be considered as micro credit products and this amount could be gradually increased up to Rs 40000 over a period of time.

Micro-credit providers through different schemes often comes with a relatively high interest rate because of the high costs of repayment collection, irregularity of loan payment and absence of securities. The loan extended to members of community-based savings, cooperatives and other finance institutions have high interest rate. The interest rates vary from 23 to 25 percent in India. Rural consumers are unable to reimburse the overall amount in which the interests represent a non-negligible amount. As a result a group based delivery model for financing of clean energy products products is advised which can be used by different members of the SHG by involvement of various financial institutions.

A group is formed by the rural consumers in the target community to offer financial services (micro savings, microcredit, micro-insurance, etc.) to themselves. Groups is composed of rural youth, or women from the local regions as they can create support structures for microenterprises and other work-based issues. This method can be the basic unit of operation for the Micro-Finance Institutions (MFIs). MFIs need to provide collateral free loans, group methodology can help in creating social collateral (peer pressure) that can effectively substitute physical collateral. In lending agreements, collateral is a borrower's pledge of specific property to a lender, to secure repayment of a loan.

The collateral serves as a lender's protection against a borrower's default and so can be used to offset the loan if the borrower fails to pay the principal and interest satisfactorily under the terms of the lending agreement.

The group approach delegates the entire financial process to the group rather than to the financial institutions. All financial activities such as savings, getting of loans, repayment of loans and record keeping is managed at the group level. In this method, 10-20 members are organised to form a group. These group members need to make regular savings of fixed amount in a common fund. The amount and frequency of savings is mutually decided by the group members.

After the successful working of such a group for some months the group is required to be linked to a financial institution for availability of credit. The financial institutions will issue loan in the name of group and whole group will be responsible for repayment. The amount of loan will depend upon the total accumulated amount of saving of the group. The group itself will select its members before acquiring a loan. Loans will be granted to selected member(s) of the group first and then to the rest of the members. Most financial institutions require a percentage of the loan that is supposed to be saved in advance, which points out the ability to make regular payments and serve as collateral. Group members themselves will decide about the criteria of dividing the loan among their group members. With this loan the whole group may jointly start a micro-enterprise or the members may start their individual businesses.

An individual may also use his loan for consumptive purpose or meeting other priority needs. Group members will be jointly accountable for the repayment of each other's loan and will usually meet weekly to collect repayments. To ensure repayment, peer pressure and joint liability needs to work well.

The entire group will be disqualified and will not be eligible for further loans, even if one member of the group becomes a defaulter. The creditworthiness of the borrower will therefore be determined by the members. This type of group based delivery method can help to empower the group members because they will remain involve in various group activities. They will visit the bank, market and undertake group meetings which would help them to increase self-confidence. This model will help in self-sustaining of the group and will also act as an effective monitoring mechanism for repayment of loans, for the products and services they buy.

8.2 Entrepreneurial-cum- SHG Model

In order to create an entrepreneurial-driven market for clean energy products a model has been devised called entrepreneurial-cum-SHG model for clean energy products intervention into the rural areas through the SHG, cooperative.

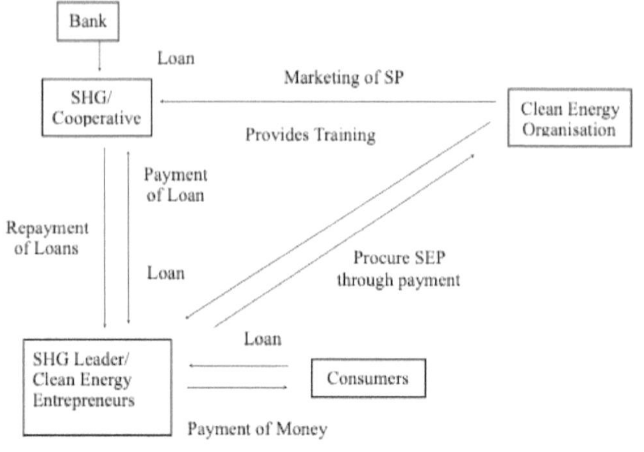

Fig 8.1: Entrepreneurial-cum- SHG Model

Here, we need to understand how a SHG, which is a community based organisation can help in marketing of any clean energy products in the rural areas. Any SHG group consist of 5-10 members that identify possible initiatives to be undertaken for the development of the livelihood in local context specific. The members in the SHGs are like minded group and consist of farmers, vendors, street hawkers, etc. who live in close vicinity to each other and can avail many schemes related to bank and others. Sometimes bank become reluctant to lend them loans to poor households for any clean energy products, for instance for the use of solar home lighting systems. Bank worries over the defaults and the high transaction costs associated with the small sized loans. For the same SHG can play an important role by bridging between the consumers and the bank.

In this model, the clean energy organisation approaches to an SHG to market their products, whether in form of an CSR initiative or from marketing perspective. The SHG leader who acts as a Clean Energy Entrepreneur (CEE) must be trained by the clean energy organisation to provide technical, managerial support to the consumers. Now, if the bank provide loans to SHG (here CEE needs to identify and submit loan proposals which can be finally sanctioned by the bank manager, before the loans are granted, more time and effort should be spend for training the SHGs members on banking habits, policies and how to maintain the books of accounts) then they would meet with the SHG members on a weekly basis who would pay the loan in instalments. The interest rates depends upon the bank which provides the loan to the SHG. Training sessions can be given to each SHG at the field level quarterly or semi-annually.

The important aspects of this model is that once the loans are provided to the SHGs, they can conduct meetings on weekly basis or every 15 days with the members, where instalments are collected. Conducting such weekly meetings can be a check against the default members and subsequently it creates a platform for a discussion. This model not only can offer an easy finance but also SHG members can deposit a nominal fee with SHG leader so as to promote banking habits. The socio-economic benefits is that the by the use of clean energy products people can advance in their secondary sources of livelihood.

From entrepreneurial perspective now if the loan is provided to the CEE directly through the bank, then the CEE can procure the Solar Products (SP) from the clean energy organisations, companies and market it to the members, or generate possible leads, subsequently going for selling of the product. Consumers can take loans from the SHG through CEE (who is also a member of the SHG) and he/she constantly monitor the actual utilisation of all types of loans to prevent non-payments or any diversion.

For this purpose, a clean energy programme card can be prepared for keeping the track of payment of instalments. Two cards can be prepared and one card will be maintained with the CEE and the other card will be kept by the consumer, bearing the same serial number. Duration for the loan of any clean energy product (like solar light, solar operated irrigation pump, solar dryer, etc.) can be kept for a short term period say 6-8 months depending on the interest and other terms and conditions of the bank. Consumers need to pay the amount within the particular time period.

8.2.1 Pay-as-You-Go (PAYG) Model

Another model for clean energy product marketing in the rural areas can be through Pay-as-You-Go (PAYG) business model. Here the consumers make a small deposit for the installation of the product and then pay regular instalments through mobile payment systems. It will have two main approaches that is energy as service approach, where the consumer pays for the electricity provided and does own the product and other approach is lease-to-own model, where the consumer becomes the owner of the product after a period of time. Out of these two models, lease-to-own is the most appropriate one. Two of the possible models has been recommended for clean energy product marketing.

In this model the consumer pays a downpayment for the product, which is attached to the smart meter. Regular payment has to be made by the consumer, if the consumer is unable to pay the amount than it will defer. The credit recharge, the payment point sends the consumer identification and recharge information to the service provider and it sends a recharge code. Then, the consumer uses this recharge code to unlock the system and gets the energy credits, further allowing the consumer to use the system till the energy credit gets exhausted. After the completion of 28 months the system permanently unlocks and the system is owned by the consumer. The meter locks the system after the consumer energy credit have run out.

Another possible model where the consumer purchases the clean energy product by paying some initial amount and takes the system and installs it. Consumer uses the system till the energy credits are exhausted, when finished the consumer brings the system attached to the charge controller to the service provider, where the provider attached the dongle to his/ her mobile and transfers the energy credits pertaining to the amount paid by the consumer. Dongle gets updated and the recharge is done. The consumer plugs the dongle into the charge controller and the system gets activated. This process goes on till full payment for the system is done and the system gets unlock for lifetime of the product.

8.2.2 Product Sharing Model

The product sharing model where the rural consumers when cannot afford high priced product even if they need it, they can share it with other consumers who wants to use the same product. For example the use of a clean energy operated drip irrigation system by farmers for irrigating their fields. The system given in rent with a specific amount, per hour basis or on day basis. This business model can acts as an income generation activity for the farmer, repayment of loans and subsequently helping leading him to a better quality of life. For any model to be successful it is required to build a partnership between companies and institutions, distributors, dealers, SHG members, cooperatives etc. for an effective distribution of products and services into the rural areas.

8.3 Survey for Marketing of Clean Energy Products in South Odisha and Implementation

A survey was conducted in the areas of South Odisha preferably the districts of Koraput, Nabarangapur and Malkanagiri. Samples were collected from Jeypur, Kotpad, Kundra, Boipariguda, and Koraput blocks of Koraput district. Similarly samples were also collected from Papadahandi, Chatahandi and Nabarangapur blocks of Nabarangapur district and Mathili block of Malkanagiri district. About 120 respondents were taken into account for this survey.

From the survey it was found that 63 percent of the respondents depended on the agricultural activity for their livelihood. Rest of the respondents undertook various activities such as livestock, forestry, tailoring, carpentry, etc. Forty one percent of the respondents were members of a cooperative, operating locally. About, 72 percent of the respondents were having a BPL card. From the survey it was found that 59 percent of the respondents did not have electricity at their homes and were facing the problem of lighting. Although 41 percent of the respondents were having electricity connection but they were facing the problem of fluctuation and low voltage due to which they were not getting a continuous supply of electricity during evening hours. Almost all respondents used kerosene for lighting purpose at home. Five percent of the respondents used 1 ltr, 26 percent used 2 ltr 31 percent used 3 ltr, 26 percent used 4 ltr, 7 percent used 5 ltr and 5 percent used 6 ltr of kerosene on each day for lighting, cooking and other activity during evening time. From the survey it was also found that about 83 percent of the respondents were not able to carry out any activity due to lighting problem and 69 percent of them required good lighting for at least 8 hours from evening till dawn of next day.

From the survey it was also found about 74 percent of the respondents did not have any idea about solar lighting and about 73 percent of them were interested to know about solar operated lighting. It was also found that, about 17 percent of the respondents could buy solar light with the range from Rs 1000-2000, 58 percent from Rs 2000-3000, 18 percent from Rs 3000-4000 and 7 percent from Rs 4000-5000. After undertaking the survey a model was initiated for marketing of the clean energy products. The model of Entrepreneurial-cum- SHG model was adopted for use of clean energy products.

Here, the SHG members helped in marketing of any clean energy product into the rural areas. SHG members identified possible initiatives to be undertaken for the development of the livelihood in local context specific. The members in the SHGs were like minded group and consist of farmers, vendors, street hawkers, etc. who lived in close vicinity to each other. They availed many schemes related to bank and others. Sometimes bank was reluctant to lend loans them for clean energy products, for instance for the use of solar home lighting systems. Bank worried over the defaults and the high transaction costs associated with the small sized loans. For the same SHG played an important role by bridging between the members and the bank.

In this model, the clean energy organisation, here the Auroville Energy Products (AEP) approached to the SHG to market their products. The SHG leader who acts here as a Clean Energy Entrepreneur (CEE) was trained by AEP to provide technical, managerial support to the consumers.

Bank provided loans to SHG and they meet with the SHG members on a weekly basis who paid the loan in instalments. The interest rates depended on the bank which provided the loan to the SHG. Training sessions were given to each SHG at the field level on a quarterly. The important aspects of this model was that once the loans were provided to the SHG, they conducted meetings on weekly basis with the members, where instalments were collected. Conducting such weekly meetings helped in checking the default members and subsequently it created a platform for a discussion. This helped not only for an easy finance but also SHG members could deposit a nominal fee with SHG leader so as to promote banking habits. The socio-economic benefits was that the by the use of clean energy products members could advance in their secondary sources of livelihood.

For this purpose, a clean energy programme card was prepared for keeping the track of payment of instalments. Two cards can be prepared and one card was maintained with the CEE and the other card was kept by the member, bearing the same serial number. Duration for the loan of the product (like solar light, solar operated irrigation pump, solar dryer, etc.) kept for a short term period of 6 months depending on the interest and other terms and conditions of the bank. Members paid the amount within the particular time period.

8.4 Conclusion

Although there are different models still prevailing in rural India for marketing of clean energy products, here a snapshot of models prevailing in rural Odisha and in South Odisha in particular was undertaken. The Entrepreneurial-cum- SHG model was adopted in rural context for marketing of clean energy products in rural areas of South

Odisha. Next chapter focuses on sustainable energy irrigation model for enhancing livelihood security in rural areas of South Odisha.

CHAPTER NINE

SUSTAINABLE ENERGY IRRIGATION MODEL FOR ENHANCING LIVELIHOOD IN SOUTH ODISHA

This chapter focuses on the diffusion of cycle mounted solar operated irrigation system in the region of South of Odisha. A case study analysis has been adopted to understand the diffusion process of cycle mounted solar operated irrigation system. Factors were found out which helped in diffusion of the irrigation system in South Odisha. The case is related to Kundra and Jeypur block of Koraput district of South Odisha. The study was undertaken by a cooperative, Pataneswari Agricultural Cooperative Society and Centurion University based at the city of Jeypore and Bhubaneswar in the state of Odisha and an action research approach was adopted. This chapter has three section. The first section, focuses on a the study area along with the process flow for sustainable energy irrigation. Second section focuses on the methodology and third section focuses on impact of use of cycle mounted solar operated irrigation system and power interest matrix of sustainable energy irrigation model for enhancing livelihood.

India has about 21 million irrigation pumps, of which more then 9 million pumps runs on diesel and another 12 million runs on electricity (Narale et al., 2013). Electricity consumption by irrigation pumps alone, consumes about 15 percent of the India's total electricity consumption (ibid). These irrigation pumps are less efficient as well. Undertaking a grid connected system will also be too expensive as the rural households are located in a far away distance. Even if the fuel is available, it is difficult to transport to remote rural areas, other than poor physical infrastructure. The use of solar operated water pumping system or solar pumps is an attractive option here (Yu et al., 2011). Transportation of these systems will be easy, convenient as it can be transported in pieces and again reassembled on the site. It requires low maintenance, low labour, no fuel cost and pumps water when needed (ibid). Solar operated water pumping system will provide a better sustainable alternative option to fulfil irrigation requirement for agriculture purpose.

South Odisha is basically a hard rock, hilly area, with scanty and uneven rainfall. There is absence of irrigation facility and farmers in the those area face difficulty in harvesting a good yield in the Khariff season and there is hardly any scope for raising crops in Rabi season (Activity Report, 2017-18, Dept. Agriculture, Government of Odisha). In the view of providing solutions to the people, a cooperative named "Pataneswari Agriculture Cooperative Society (PACS)" along with Tata Trust and Centurion University took the initiative to design and develop a cycle mounted solar operated irrigation system. The details of the diffusion study is described in the subsequent sections.

9.1 About the Study

This study was undertaken in Jeypur and Kundra blocks of Koraput district. It consist of 22 and 12 gram panchayats, with 125 and 85 villages respectively. Whole of the population of these two blocks resides in rural areas (Census, 2011). With about 98 percent of the people of Jeypur and Kundra blocks depending on agriculture, we're facing the problem of water crises for irrigating their fields. In order to provide solution to it, a cycle mounted solar operated irrigation system was designed and developed to help the farmers and bringing in livelihood security in the region. This system used a PENTAIR DC operated submersible pump of 0.25 HP, with maximum head of 70 m head, with a discharge of 310 LPH. The system uses 2 solar panels of 175 W producing about 4.1 amp current. The system was used in a open dug well, with a overhead tank to store water. The solar panels were mounted on the carrier of the bicycle for easy movement from one farmer's field to another. This system is basically used for irrigating small patch of land used for cultivation of vegetables.

Member farmer of cooperative used this system. It was provided at Rs 25000 and was bought by the farmers from Heruguda village of Kundura block of Koraput district initially. Through this initiative, defunct bore wells (due to unavailability of electricity) was revived for irrigation and the member farmer went for year-round vegetable production, thus enhancing his income as well. Here the cooperative took loan of Rs 2 lac from State Bank of India (SBI) to facilitate the promotion of cycle mounted solar operated irrigation system to other member farmers. The system was provided to other member farmers on instalment basis. Farmers took the system and rented the system to other farmers as well which helped them in improving of their income. The Community Service Providers (CSP) were trained on technical and managerial aspects provided by Centurion University. Further the CSPs went on in giving training to other members farmers on installation, repair and maintenance of the system. Use of the system was considered as a ray of hope for the rural farmers having limited resources. Farmers, who had closely seen their crops dying due to scarcity of water, unavailability of electricity started using the system to ensure at least two-season crops in their field. Focused group discussion was carried out with the member farmers of the cooperative for understanding the impact of use of cycle mounted solar operated irrigation system. It has been discussed later in later part of this paper. Below is the small case study described of a tribal farmer from Heruguda village of Kundura block of Koraput district of South Odisha.

Krushna, of Heruguda village got benefited by using cycle mounted solar operated irrigation system. He was a tribal farmer who owned a tiny piece of land measuring 0.25 acre. In the past, he depended on rain-fed agriculture and could grow vegetables only during the rainy season. After paying for seeds, seedlings, fertilizer and pesticides, his net annual income from agriculture was Rs 6600. After getting a demonstration of the system by CSP, he agreed to take a loan and adopted it for growing vegetables in his field.

To start with, he invested further in this system and spent money on purchasing trellis, vegetable seeds, fertilizer and pesticides. The total investment amounted to Rs 60000. Since water was available on a regular basis, he was able to raise a nursery in his field. At the end of the first season, he was able to increase the production significantly and earned Rs 13700. He could further go for the second and third crops within the year. After deducting for the money spent on seeds and fertilizer, he was able to earn Rs 33350 after the second season and Rs 31000 from the third season. After paying off the capital borrowed for the system, he was left with a net earning of Rs 18600, which was about 3 times higher than what he earned in the past. In the next year he invested Rs 12000 for wire-mesh fencing around his plot on remembering the loss due to cattle grazing in previous years. Further he rented his system on an hourly basis to other farmers who would seen their crops dying due to scarcity of water and electricity, helping him in earning more and securing his livelihood. In relation with the application of the framework a process flow has been devised figure 9.1.

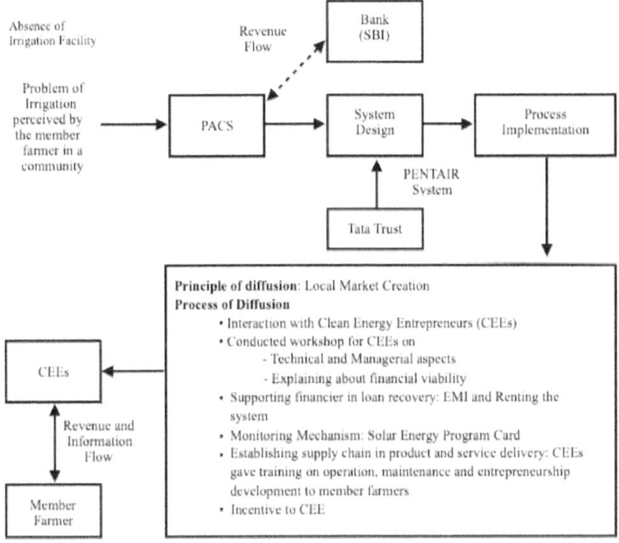

Figure 9.1: Process Flow for Sustainable Energy
Irrigation

From the figure 9.1, the bank, SBI provided loan to
Pataneswari Agriculture Cooperative Society (PACS) and
Tata Trusts provided the pump and the system was
designed and developed in Centurion University. The
major role was played by the implementing agency (PACS)
in implementation aspect and Centurion University in
designing aspect. Factors such as cost of the product,
payment through EMI, portability of the product, renting
the product, easy to operate, repair and maintenance by
CSP and asset creation for the member farmer were some
of the important factors which helped for the diffusion to
take place. There was a need for a strong technical service

partner to last mile connectivity which was fulfilled by the presence of a godown or a warehouse with the availability of spares parts of the DC pump, provision of training to CSPs on service, repair and maintenance and a designated toll free number for quick and better service was also put in place. Involvement of all these actors and factors helped in the diffusion to take place.

9.2 Methodology

The major role was played by the implementing agency, PACS, facilitating institution, Harsha Trust and technical partner, Centurion University. For successful diffusion and implementation, interaction was held with the CSPs of the cooperative. With farmers facing the problem of water, and unable to irrigate their fields, they saw their crops dying. Member farmers approached the CSPs in a motive to get the solution. As a result, CSPs discussed this problem of member farmers with the officials of the cooperative. In the view of solving the problem, PACS approached the bank and applied for the loan for designing and development of a cycle mounted solar operated irrigation system. The reason for using a cycle mounted design was mainly because of its portability and ease of use from one field to field. Further the loan was availed by the bank with a payable interest to PACS. Several meetings were held between the CSPs and the PACS officials. Design for cycle mounted solar operated irrigation system was done by the researcher at Centurion University with the support from Tata Trust by providing the DC pump. After successful design and experiment it was provided to PACS. PACS provided the system to the member farmer, to be used in the fields for irrigation.

Training was provided by the researcher from Centurion University and Harsha Trust, in the local language to the CSPs on the advantages of using a cycle mounted solar operated irrigation system. After completion of the training program, the CSPs trained the member farmer on how to manage and operate the product. An incentive mechanism was placed by PACS. Incentive was only given when the entire instalment for the product was recovered and paid to the cooperative.

For purchasing the system it was difficult for the member farmer to access the capital at the initial stage. For solving the problem, members were provided with easy financing options by payment on EMI basis, where the member farmer purchased the system with a minimum amount and rest amount was to be paid in instalment basis. Some member farmers used this system as rent to other farmers who were facing the problem of irrigating their fields. Renting the system, helped the farmers in paying their instalment in a easy way.

The major hurdle was, ensuring quality after-sale at minimum effort and with less time. For achieving the same, technical training was provided to CSPs on how to carry out repair and maintenance of the cycle mounted solar operated irrigation system. They provided after-sales service for the product in quick time. A designated toll free number was in place for helping the member farmer for quick and service delivery. The drip irrigation system model is given in the figure 9.2, to enhance the skill knowledge of the farmers and traines.

Figure 9.2: Basic Solar Drip Irrigation System Model

With quick service, availability of system on EMI options, portability and renting the system, cycle mounted solar operated irrigation system was used by member farmers of the cooperative. Initially only one member farmer used the system but later, 40 cycle mounted solar operated irrigation systems were bought by other member farmers as well. Apart from the above figures, till date about 730 number of cycle mounted solar operated irrigation system are being used by farmers at different locations of South Odisha, given in the figure 9.3.

Figure 9.3: Cycle Mounted Solar Powered Irrigation System

The above cycle mounted solar powered irrigation system consists of Solar modules (40 W each), Charge controller (12 V, 4 A), Water pump (0.5 HP), Cycle, Mechanical structure and Electrical appliances.

9.3 Impact of Use of Cycle Mounted Solar Operated Irrigation System

This section focuses on the impact of use of cycle mounted solar operated irrigation system on the members of the cooperative. To know the impact of use of cycle mounted solar operated irrigation system, focused group discussions was held with the member farmers of the cooperative with the involvement of CSPs and CEO of PACS office based at Jeypore, a small town based in South Odisha.

Initially only one member, who was also a CSP of the cooperative from Heruguda village of Kundura block purchased the cycle mounted solar operated irrigation system. He used the system in his field and gave it as rent to other member farmers. Gradually the member farmers showed interest in buying the system and approached PACS. Focused group discussion was held with the member farmers who were using the system and they shared their experience of using the system.

Focused group discussion was held with the member farmers from Boipariguda village of Boipariguda tehsil in the PACS office. They had to walk to near by water source to fetch water in buckets from the dam site to irrigate their fields to grow different vegetables such as cabbage, brinjal, tomatoes etc. It was taking almost 5 hours starting from fetching of water to irrigation, leaving less time for other essential work such as hoeing, weeding and tending in addition to household chores. With much difficulty they arranged a diesel pump for pumping water from near by pond but later they could not afford the rising fuel cost, along with the problem in transporting. Eventually the pump broke down and they did not use it further. Later, after discussion with the CSPs and getting a demonstration of the system, and knowing that the system can be purchased through EMI options, they all agreed to purchase the system. Presently they now use the system and fill the tanks each day at mid-day to water their fields in less time. The system was easy to operate, portable and was quick in functioning. They informed that, with the use of the system they are now able to irrigate their fields and grow different vegetables.

Focused group discussion was held with the member farmers from Kaliagam village of Jeypur tehsil. They told that the system was very easy to operate, and does not require any complex technical knowledge. Further, as the system was cycle mounted it was easy for transport from one field to another, leading to reduction in drudgery.

Another focused group discussion was held with the member farmers from Bhusangaguda village of Kundura tehsil. They started using the system for irrigation in their fields and grew different vegetables. Earlier they were growing only one variety of vegetable, but later they started growing different vegetables and spices through inter-cropping and attaching drip pipes to the system. It resulted in water savings, improved seed germination and high yield. With high yield, now they sell the spices and vegetables in local market. This has led to availability of spices and vegetables when ever they required. They now even sell these items in local haat which has helped them in increase of their income.

Focused group discussion was also held with all the members of the cooperative who were using both solar operated lights and cycle mounted solar operated irrigation system. From the discussion it was found that the impact of using the products was same which has been discussed earlier. The community level interactions substantiate that the use of solar operated lights and cycle mounted solar operated irrigation system used by all the 105 members of the cooperative has helped in enhancing their quality of life, given in the figure

9.3.1 Power Interest Matrix of Sustainable Energy Irrigation Model for Enhancing Livelihood

From the case study and implementation process, discussed we have recognised various actors. These actors are Pataneswari agriculture cooperative society (PACS), Bank (SBI), Tata Trust, Centurion University, Clean energy entrepreneurs and member farmers. Here the actors are the stakeholders. Here stakeholders are both the people and organisations. Table 9.1 shows the power-interest matrix for actors of sustainable energy irrigation model for enhancing livelihood.

Table 9.1: Power Interest Table for Actors of Sustainable Energy Irrigation Model for Enhancing Livelihood

Actors	Power-Interest Category
Member Farmers	High power- High interest
PACS	High power-High interest
Bank	Low power-High interest
Tata Trust	Low power-High interest
Centurion University	Low power-High interest
CSPs	High power- High interest

From the case study, it is found that member farmers of the cooperative were the consumers of solar operated irrigation system. They were facing the problem of irrigating their fields. Being the consumers, they were highly interested in adopting this product in order to save their crops. The member farmers have high power in influencing the diffusion process, as they were the key decision makers in adopting the product.

PACS had high power in influencing the decision making process as the members were part of PACS itself and was interested in opening a clean energy vertical through the use of clean energy products where they could provide clean energy solutions to their member farmers. Bank on the other hand had low power as they were only interested in providing loan to PACS in payable interest. Tata Trusts had low power in influencing the diffusion process, but were highly interested in focusing on rural development through sustainable manner. They also provided the pump for the system as well. Centurion University had also low power in influencing the diffusion process, but was highly interested in uplifting the quality of life of the rural people. They designed the system and conducted many experiments before providing the system to PACS. They provided training to the CSPs on the advantages of using a cycle mounted solar operated irrigation system, other technical and managerial aspects. Apart from it, they also designed the monitoring mechanism for easy payment of the system. Community Service Providers had high power and high interest in the diffusion process. They act as a leader in influencing and motivating the member farmers to adopt clean energy products and drove the diffusion process forward. With the incentive mechanism in place, they were highly interested in venturing into solar business and and thus became Clean Energy Entrepreneurs (CEEs).

9.4 Conclusion

From the study some factors were found out which are necessary for diffusion of cycle mounted solar operated irrigation system in the rural areas. Use of local resource, involvement of cooperative was very much essential for the diffusion to take place. Lastly, all the stakeholders coordinated, cooperate and collaborated with each other so as to achieve diffusion of solar lights in the areas of Kundra and Jeypur tehsil of South Odisha. This not only led to the diffusion of cycle mounted solar operated irrigation system but also was accompanied with service delivery as well. It also helped in enhancement of quality of life of rural people. Next chapter focuses on a clean energy product, called solar operated agri-pesticide sprayer

SIMULATION OF A SOLAR OPERATED AGRI PESTICIDE SPRAYER USING PVSYST SOFTWARE

This chapter focuses on clean energy product called solar operated agri pesticide sprayer using PVSYST software. This chapter focuses on design and development of agri pesticide sprayer using a simulation software. This chapter has two sections. The first section focuses on the literature review and the second section focuses on analysis and results and discussions.

Accesses to modern energy services are necessary for improved health and agricultural productivity (UNDP, 2001). In the present chapter a smart agri pesticide sprayer was developed which was operated by solar power. It is efficient as compared to conventional sprayer which is operated on diesel and requires less time for spraying larger area and it also reduce back pain. The main components of the system includes solar panel, charge controller, battery, DC pump, and nozzle with sprayer. The entire system is analyzed by PV syst software.

All of the world's problems can be solved with energy. It contributes to the human and economic growth of any area, state, or country. In today's world, energy access is a prevalent issue. Access to clean energy can aid in the development of rural tribal communities. "Electrification is linked to a range of development improvements, such as increasing in income, generating employment, and achieving better health and education" (Barron and Torero, 2017; Chakravorty et al. 2016). In recent era, the demand of electricity has raised drastically. In order to overcome that smart agri sprayer had fabricated which consist of solar panel, battery, charge controller, DC pump, and sprayer. It is easy to install, operate and maintain and diesel was not required. The development of sprayer has following objectives. It is operated by clean energy which is pollution free with less maintenance cost.

10.1 Literature Review

S. charvani et al., had develop a sprayer which is operated by solar panel, battery and pump. R.Joshua et al., develop a sprayer for discharging pesticide and is operated through a DC motor. Harshit Jain et al. and E. Zahab et al., designed a solar water pumping system which consists of three speed controller and MPPT device for charging and discharging battery. Nithin Vasanth et al., carried out an experimental work on solar powered sprayer and all data had been submitted through GSM. Yallappa D et al., had develop a multipurpose solar operated sprayer. Kohle had done a experimental work solar water pumping by using manual tracking system.

10.2 Experimental Set Up and Diagram of Spraying System

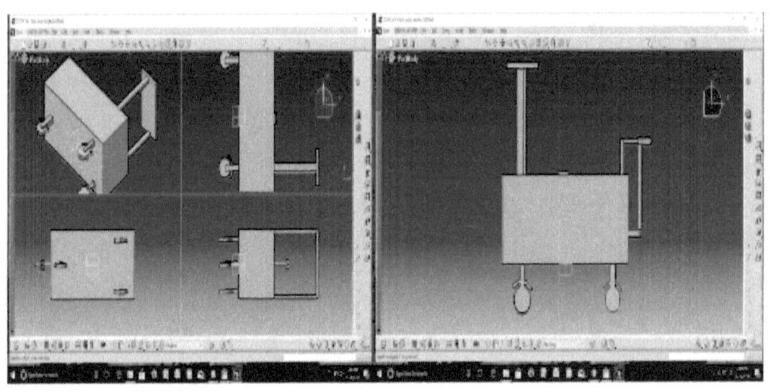

Figure 10.1: Modeling of Spraying System by Catia Software

10.2.1 Analysis by using PVSYST Software

By considering simulation parameter such as geographical data of Bhubaneswar, Odisha location, system parameters (sizing of solar panel and battery), used energy, performance ratio, loss of head were obtained. In the figure 10.2 it has been shown below.

SHIV, BIJAYA B. NAYAK, DEBASHREE, ADARSH, ANUP, SOUMYA,
SASMITA, BONITA, AKANKSHYA, MONALISHA

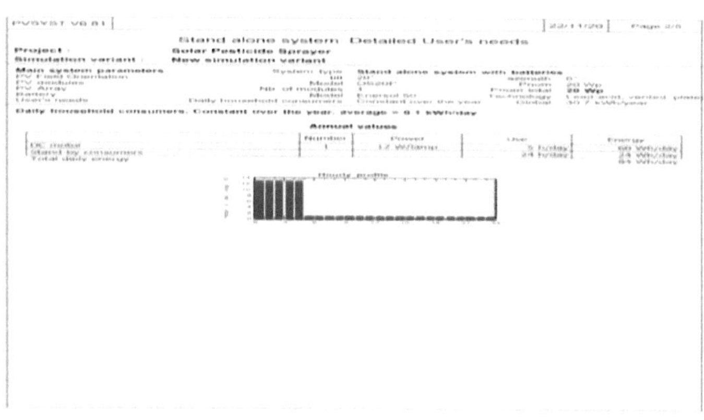

PVSYST V6.81		22/11/20	Page 3/5

Stand alone system: Main results

Project :   **Solar Pesticide Sprayer**

Simulation variant :   **New simulation variant**

Main system parameters

	System type	**Stand alone system with batteries**	
PV Field Orientation	tilt 20°	azimuth	0°
PV modules	Model OS20P	Pnom	20 Wp
PV Array	Nb. of modules 1	Pnom total	**20 Wp**
Battery	Model Enersol 50	Technology	Lead-acid, vented, plate
User's needs	Daily household consumers	Constant over the year Global	30.7 kWh/year

Main simulation results

System Production	**Available Energy**	**23.55 kWh/year**	Specific prod.	1177 kWh/kWp/year
	Used Energy	21.14 kWh/year	Excess (unused)	0.00 kWh/year
	Performance Ratio PR	56.69 %	Solar Fraction SF	68.94 %
Loss of Load	Time Fraction	31.3 %	Missing Energy	9.52 kWh/year
Battery ageing (State of Wear)	Cycles SOW	95.4%	Static SOW	80.0%
	Battery lifetime	5.0 years		

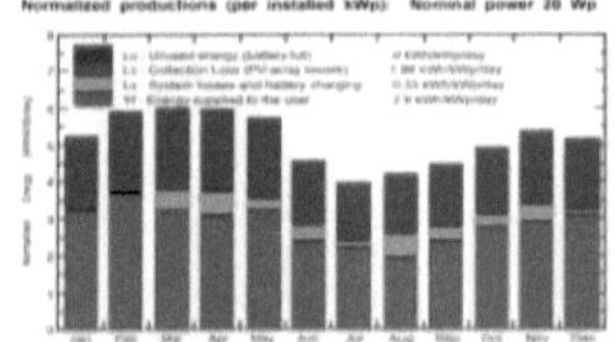
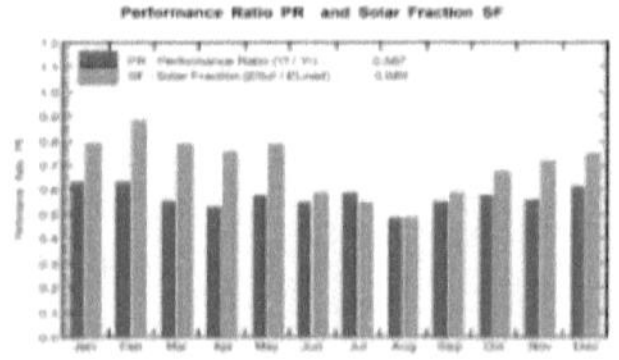

New simulation variant
Balances and main results

	GlobHor	GlobEff	E_Avail	EUnused	E_Miss	E_User	E_Load	SolFrac
	kWh/m²	kWh/m²	kWh	kWh	kWh	kWh	kWh	
January	132.5	158.7	2.073	0.000	0.563	2.041	2.604	0.784
February	141.7	160.8	2.092	0.000	0.291	2.061	2.352	0.876
March	173.3	182.0	2.355	0.000	0.571	2.033	2.604	0.781
April	180.5	174.5	2.260	0.000	0.638	1.882	2.520	0.747
May	188.2	172.1	2.225	0.000	0.570	2.034	2.604	0.781
June	146.6	132.0	1.706	0.000	1.042	1.478	2.520	0.587
July	129.9	117.8	1.520	0.000	1.186	1.418	2.604	0.545
August	134.4	126.1	1.626	0.000	1.354	1.250	2.604	0.480
September	130.9	130.2	1.688	0.000	1.046	1.474	2.520	0.585
October	138.3	148.3	1.931	0.000	0.859	1.745	2.604	0.670
November	131.7	157.4	2.045	0.000	0.733	1.787	2.520	0.709
December	127.0	155.9	2.026	0.000	0.672	1.932	2.604	0.742
Year	1754.8	1815.9	23.546	0.000	9.524	21.130	30.660	0.689

Legends:	GlobHor	Horizontal global irradiation	E_Miss	Missing energy
	GlobEff	Effective Global, corr. for IAM and shadings	E_User	Energy supplied to the user
	E_Avail	Available Solar Energy	E_Load	Energy need of the user (Load)
	EUnused	Unused energy (battery full)	SolFrac	Solar fraction (EUsed / ELoad)

SHIV, BIJAYA B. NAYAK, DEBASHREE, ADARSH, ANUP, SOUMYA,
SASMITA, BONITA, AKANKSHYA, MONALISHA

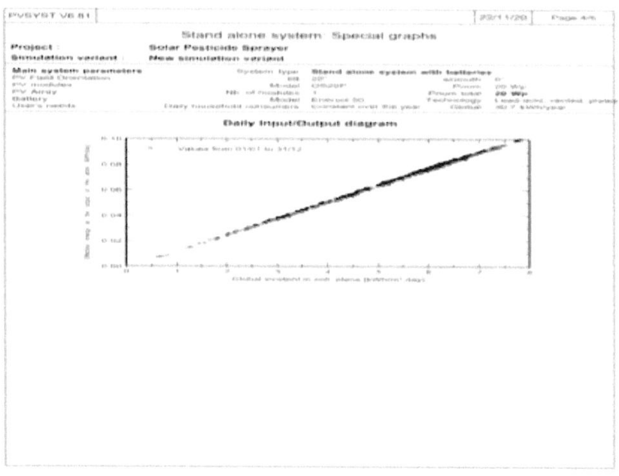

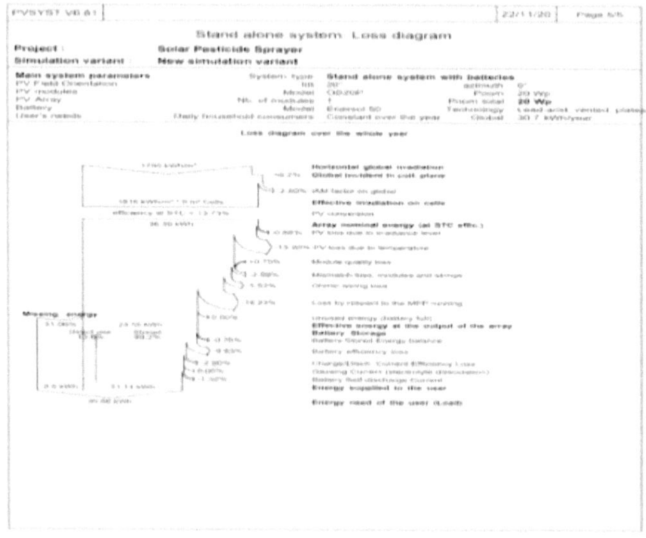

Figure 10.2: Analysis Report by using PVSYST Software

10.3 Results and Discussions

10.3.1 Power Conversion Efficiency of the Panel

η=Maximum power/Minimum power= output power/ input power Where,

Under STD condition

Irradiance = 1000 W/m²

Area of solar cell =0.4m x 0.4m

Input power = 160 W

Output power = Voc x Isc x FF

Voc = 21.5, Isc= Short circuit current= 1.29

10.3.2 File factor (FF)

The output in the solar panel is not 100%. So it is the resistance in the solar panel. FF= loss due to file factor = (Voc-ln (Voc+0.72))/ (Voc+1). FF= 81.7%

Output power = open circuit voltage x short circuit current x Fill factor = 22.6 W

η = output power / input power = 14 % which power conversion efficiency

η =(? x ? x ? x ??)/(Voc x Isc) = 0.36 =36%

Figure 10.3: Testing Operation

10.4 Conclusion

From the above experiment, it was found that maximum discharge rate at outlet of DC pump was found to be 4.3 lit/min by taking solar panel of 20W; battery capacity of 12V, 7.2Ah; charge controller of 12V, 10A; DC Pump of 12V, 4.2 lph. It is a cost effective system as compared to other systems. It can be used for multipurpose task such as for charging mobile, operating LED lights, etc. With a battery backup it can be used both during evening and a in cloudy weather.

Next chapter focuses on a clean energy product, called solar operated box type cooker.

CHAPTER ELEVEN

PERFORMANCE TESTING OF A SOLAR BOX TYPE COOKER

This chapter focuses on design and development of a solar box type cooker. It has two sections. The first section focuses on the literature review and the second section focuses on experimental setup, results and discussions.

Generally in rural areas, people prepare food by using conventional methods such as a *Chulha* which emits fumes and harmful gases, which causes respiratory problem. The main component of the cooker comprises of a folding type reflector which is made up of Aluminium with a highly glazing material, that reflects radiation and focus it into the cooking chamber. There were six numbers of reflectors which are integrated and it focuses incidentally radiations individually to one point so that heating effect is increased. The present system is low in weight, portaable and easy to use. The maximum temperature was found to be 100 degree centigrade and cooking power and standard cooking power were found to be 17.5 W and 17.09 W respectively which is sufficient enough for cooking.

Due to increase in population, there is demand for good quality of life. Due to less reservation of fossil fuel, environmental concern, there is a transition from unclean energy to clean energy. Clean energy can contribute significantly in enhancing domestic and industrial economies. Due to unreliable availability of electricity and use of conventional cook stoves, the present chapter aims for developing an alternative cleaned energy product for rural development.

11.1 Literature Review

S. Geddam et al., designed a box type solar cooker with parameters such as optical efficiency and heat capacity. Undertaking characteristic graphs a comparision was carried out with predicted values and compared values. Finned type cooking vessel was used so as to reduce the time factor. Similarly, J. Folaranmi et al., had designed a double glazed type solar cooker and standard cooking power was estimated.

Z. Ademe et al., designed a box type cooker with glazing wiper mechanism and standard cooking power and cumulative efficiency was calculated. Simulation was carried out to calculate inner wall temperature distribution.

G.Palanikumar et al., designed a natural box type cooker with fuzzy technique. The overall efficiency was found to be 15.4 percent.

M.Balakrishnan et al., had designed a parabolic solar cooker used for generating steam. H. Terres et al., had designed a cooker with internal reflector. A temperature sensor and solar meter were used to measure temperature and solar radiation. L.B. Sosa et al., designed a solar cooker for rural people which helped in reduction of the consumption of timber fuels as well as reducing respiratory diseases.

11.2 Experimental Set Up

The figure 11.1 shows the experimental set up of solar cooker which consists of folding type of reflector, transparent or cover plate and absorbing plate. There were six numbers of reflectors made up of Aluminium materials with a glazing, 3 mm thickness sheet, integrated with each other and fixed on the top of the cooker.

The main reason of taking six number of reflectors is to achieve maximum incident radiation, to focus on a single point. The transparent plate was made up of tempered glass which is used to reflect the incident radiation to absorbing plate. The interior area of the cooker was black painted along with the absorbing plate so as to absorb maximum radiation and convert into heat.

The box is made in slope angle of 200 and it faced towards south. At the bottom of cooker, glass wool of 1 inch is fixed in order to reduce heat loss and it act as an insulator. The bottom dimension of of the cooker stands at 16 inch×16 inch, front dimension at 16×8.5 inches, back side of the cooker stands at 16×12.5 inches, glass dimensions is 16×16 inches and dimension of reflector is 17.5 ×19.75 inches.

Figure 11.1. Experimental set up of Solar Box Type of Cook. (1). Transparent or cover plate, (2) Reflector(4 numbers), (3).Temperature sensor, (4) Lux meter. Figure 2 . The interior part of the cooking chamber painted black.

11.3 Results and Discussions

The performance of solar cooker can be tested by placing it in open area where maximum solar radiation is available and without shadow effect. The cooker was placed towards south direction. The temperature was measured through a temperature sensor fixed inside the cooker in regular intervals. At the same time solar radiation was also measured with the help of lux meter. For testing purpose the water is taken. The table 11.1 represents the testing data of cooker in a sunny day.

Table 11.1: Testing Data of Cooker in a Sunny Day

Si no	Timing (AM/PM)	Temperature in 0_c	Intensity of solar radiation in LUX
1	09:30AM	85	71400
2	10:40 AM	90	71900
3	11:00 AM	95	72500
4	12:20PM	100	80900
5	1:00 PM	100	73600
6	2:20 PM	60	53600
7	3:30 PM	50	12300
8	4:00 PM	50	12000

The cooking power can be calculated by using the formula= Mwater× Cwater × (T2-T1)/time interval taken

Given Cwater =4.2J/g0C or 4179.6J/KgK

Putting T2= 100 C and T1=95 C, Mwater = 1 Litre,

Cooking power was calculated as 17.5 W

Similarly standard cooking power was calculated as by multiplying standard intensity of solar light = 700W/m2

[Mwater× Cwater × (T2-T1) ×700W/m2]/time interval taken× g, where g= 9.8 m/s2

Standard cooking power found =17.09 W

11.4 Conclusion

The present experimental investigation is to use the box type solar cooker, an alternative solution for conventional method of cooking. The cooker is portable, easy to use. During the experimental study the highest temperature was found to be 150 degree centigrade which was sufficient enough for boiling water or cooking food. The design of cooker can be modified by using of two numbers of cover plates in order to increase efficiency for future scope. Lastly, the next chapter covers some case study from South

Odisha accompanied with some recommendations.

CHAPTER TWELVE

CASE STUDY

Livelihood security in rural areas can be broadly divided into three categories like on-farm, non-farm and off-farm based on land use as primary criterion. Livelihood such as agricultural production depends on land. All such predominantly land dependent activities are covered under on-farm livelihood options. These include cultivation of paddy, wheat, vegetables, etc. Those livelihood activities that do not require cultivation but are of manufacturing or service category are called non-farm activities. Activities include agro-processing, transport, health, warehousing, retailing, etc. Some activities which do not require large amount of land ownership are covered under off-farm category. These include goatery, poultry, fishery, dairy, etc. They may require access to pasture for grazing, which can be a part of community or forest land. Clean energy requirement will vary on the basis of livelihood activities practiced by households in rural areas. In this chapter various cases have been discussed from rural areas of the South Odisha where there is application of clean energy products has taken place.

12.1 Use of Clean Energy for Sustainable Livelihood Security

According to Oxford Dictionary, "livelihood means a way of earning enough money to live on". Security means the "state of being secure". As per Chambers and Conway (1992), the term "livelihood means activities, entitlements and assets by which people make a living". Livelihood security deals with the "adequate stocks and flows of food and cash to meet basic needs of people" (ibid). It is the "results or outcome of the activities undertaken by rural people to lead their life" (Niehof and Price, 2001).

"Livelihood security focuses on having adequate and access to sustainable income and resources to meet and satisfy the basic needs" (Drinkwater and McEwan, 1992). It includes people's access to food, safe drinking water, health facilities, education, proper sanitation and better infrastructure (ibid).

12.1.1 The Case of Solar Operated Kiosk

Mr. Dhaneswar Majhi, a young man from Badchatrang village in Kalahandi district in South Odisha, became a Clean Energy Entrepreneur. He set up a digital kiosk to give photocopying and printing services to the residents of his gram panchayat. People had to go around 80 kilometres one way simply to acquire a rupee one photocopy. People from the SELCO Foundation visited with Dhaneswar in 2016-17 to learn about his plans and discovered that the region lacked consistent power supply to open the business. Through a MUDRA loan, SELCO Foundation and Bhawanipatna Branch of Syndicate Bank assisted Dhaneswar in opening his kiosk. The overall cost of the financial project was Rs. 1.71 lakh, of which SELCO contributed a margin of Rs. 25000 and a risk reserve of Rs. 35000. Dhaneswar paid Rs. 70000 toward the creation of the shop, and the bank offered a loan of Rs. 76500 with a 9.68 percent interest rate for 60 months. The SELCO

Foundation supplied the bank with a risk fund in order to increase banker confidence in funding the project, as well as margin money support.

12.1.2 The Case of Solar Operated Home Lighting System

Thumaul Rampur block in Kalahandi district is a rural place with limited access to essential services including as power, water, roads, transportation, and communication. Despite the fact that the grid is linked to multiple residences, there is no regular provision of energy, and connections from houses located inside a forest reserve to the grid are not established on time. This causes homes to go without power for weeks or months, especially during the monsoon season. The SELCO Foundation collaborated with the Syndicate Bank Bhawanipatna Branch and the solar firm, Mukti Solar to provide solar-powered home lighting systems to 500 homes. The household had a higher quality of life and was able to save more money because kerosene-based lighting were no longer used. The overall project cost was Rs. 41.85 lakh for 500 systems, with SELCO contributing Rs. 12.50 lakh and a risk reserve of Rs. 13.425 lakh. The margin was Rs. 2.50 lakh, and the bank offered a loan of Rs. 26.85 lakh. To encourage the habit of saving, the homes were organised into Joint Liability Groups (JLGs), and bank funding was supplied.

12.1.3 The Case of Solar Operated Sewing Machine

Mr. Ramsingh Kabadi has a tailoring shop in South Odisha's Badchatrang village, Kalahandi district. His business was doing well, and he earned between Rs. 6000 and Rs. 8000 every month. However, he was unable to meet expanding demand since he was unable to expand his business and the lack of energy prevented him from working past 5 p.m. Ramsingh was able to purchase an energy-efficient solar-powered sewing machine thanks to a MUDRA loan from the SELCO Foundation and the Syndicate Bank of Bhawanipatna Branch. The system was installed by ABHA Innovations. The CEE has grown from one to two sewing machines and employed another employee. He has also worked hard to enhance his creditworthiness by strengthening his relationship with the bank. The total cost of the project was Rs. 24185, with a profit margin of Rs. 5000. The bank granted a loan of Rs. 19185 for 28 months at an interest rate of 9.68 percent. The bank made the loan using the asset obtained as the primary security, with no further collateral.

12.1.4 The Case of Solar Urja (study) Lamp (SoUL)

Clean energy has the potential to be the alternative to energy access problem, specifically for accessing to electricity for lighting needs. Applications of clean energy products has been growing from few last years in the failure of grid electrification reaching the sparsely populated rural population. Although the range of clean energy products are many but the most preferred product is seen to be solar based systems. Use of applications of clean energy through solar based products are fast becoming preferred options in rural areas over the grid electrification mainly due its reliability.

Use of clean energy products like solar based lighting system has a positive impact on education, health and livelihoods through increased study hours of children, less exposure to use of kerosene and aiding livelihood activities. Solar based lighting has increased the study hours of children in rural areas by one and half hours. It was also found that there was a decrease in the expenditure on kerosene and electricity bill post purchasing of solar based lighting systems. Similar insights were also found the study conducted by Garg.

In order to increase the study hours of school children in rural areas in India, Indian Institute of Technology (IIT) Mumbai, along with National Clean Energy Fund (NCEF) with the support of the Ministry of New and Renewable Energy (MNRE), Government of India, endeavoured to change the lives of 1 million school children by distributing 1 million Solar Urja Lamps (clean energy product). For the same, they had developed a model called "Localisation of Solar Energy Model" through its Million Solar Urja Light (SoUL) program. In order to provide Solar Urja Lamps (SoUL), facilitating institution, financial institution, manufacturer and implementing agency came together to provide Solar Urja Lamps. The case has been discussed and actors and factors has been identified in the subsequent sections.

This study was undertaken across four Indian states of Madhya Pradesh, Maharashtra, Rajasthan, and Odisha. In Odisha, IIT Mumbai with support from facilitating institution collaborated with the implementing agency to implement this in rural areas of Nabarangpur district of South Odisha.

The system used solar PV technology with its inherent feature of providing off-grid decentralised energy at an individual or household level. This system was a study lamp for reading purpose. It had energy efficient high quality LEDs which consumed less than 0.5W, giving adequate light output with 100 degree angle by providing adjustable goose neck for flexibility in light focus. It can be used as a bed lamp after a child study and was portable. It gave long hours of lighting with reliable rechargeable nickel–metal hydride (NiMH) battery. IIT Mumbai designed the system and spares were supplied by Sirius Solar Energy Systems based at Hyderabad.

The actual cost per Solar Urja (study) Lamp (SoUL) was Rs. 500, however at the subsidised cost beneficiary contribution was Rs. 120 per lamp. Any child enrolled in the school studying between class V to class XII from un-electrified household, got Solar Urja (study) Lamp (SoUL) at a price of Rs. 120 and avail free servicing facility provided in their vicinity.

The implementing agency was supported by the facilitating institution and funding agency. Service providers (SP) of the implementing agency were trained on technical and managerial aspects by the facilitating institution. They were provided training on assembling, sales, repair and maintenance of the solar lamps which helped them to generate employment in the intervention areas. School going children were the ultimate consumers for using the solar urja lamps. It helped them to study during evening hours.

Sirius Solar Energy Systems was the manufacturer for the solar urja lamps. These kits along the spares from the manufacturer were procured by facilitating institution and were provided to the implementing agency who then assembled these kits in the lamp form and then provided it to the school going children at subsidised rate. Finance in the form of grant from Central Government, State Government, through CSR initiatives, and from other trusts were received for the activities to made this study sustainable. The actual cost of the lamp was Rs 500 (gross price at Rs 350 per lamp, contingencies and other overhead at Rs 60 per lamp, cost of assembly and incentive at Rs 60 and repair and maintenance at Rs 30 per lamp) but it was made available at subsidised rate to school going children at Rs 120. From the total cost of lamp of Rs 500, Central

Government, State Government, CSR initiatives and from other trusts contributed Rs 380 and the beneficiary paid Rs 120 per solar lamp.

IIT, Mumbai act as a facilitating institution. It facilitated the whole study, channelised the fund received from the financial institutions and provide the solar urja lamp kits, spares received from the manufacturers to the implementing agency. It selected the implementing agency and manufacturers through tender process and were shortlisted under uniform rate contract. It also collaborated with academic institutions to monitor and measure the progress of the study with the involvement of the implementing agency. The facilitating institution conducted training programs for the representatives of the implementing agency for assembly, testing, distribution and campaigning strategy to reach out to the school going children. IIT, Mumbai guided, mentored and provide handholding support to the implementing agency in implementing the program.

Harsha Trust, an NGO based at South Odisha, act as an implementing agency. It implemented the study in coordination with the facilitation institution. The implementing agency office present in the region, acts as an assembling and distribution unit for solar lamps kits and spares received from facilitation institution.

The implementing agency sent its service providers along with 9 distributors of electrical components from the local area to facilitating institution to receive training on assembly, testing, distribution and campaigning strategy for the solar lamps. The reason for sending these distributors was, they would provide repair and maintenance of solar lamps when malfunctioned.

The implementing agency also developed that training manuals, PPT, banners and leaflets, guidelines for developing the infrastructure to assemble and distribute the solar urja lamps in coordination with the facilitation institution. They provided the lamps along with the PPT, banners and leaflets to the teachers for creating awareness, motivating the students and their guardians to adopt the solar lamps. The implementing agency also received the amount provided by the teachers from the students and put it in the account of the facilitating institution and in return received the incentive from the facilitating institution.

Process implementation focuses on the diffusion process. For implementation of the diffusion process, the implementing agency implemented this study in Nabarangpur district of South Odisha. This study was undertaken in three blocks of Nabarangpur district (Nabarangpur, Papadahandi and Koshagumuda). Solar urja lamps were provided by the facilitation institution to the implementing agency. The implementing agency sold these lamps to school going children by involving the teachers from the school.

Teachers helped the implementing agency in identifying the children from un-electrified household and who receives less hours of electricity. The implementing agency conducted frequent interactions, meetings with the representatives of the facilitating institution, teachers of the school, service providers and the distributors. Awareness programs and campaigns was conducted in schools involving teachers, by the implementing agency. Teachers influenced the guardians and students to adopt the solar lamps. Live demonstration of solar urja lamps were conducted in the evening hours in order to create a sense of urge and motivating the guardians to own it.

More emphasis was given on how the use of solar lamps would help the children to read during evening hours and educating them.

Here, the service providers (SP) were from the implementing agency and distributors were identified by the implementing agency from three blocks. They were basically distributors of electrical components who would provide components of the solar lamps when malfunctioned. They were trained by the facilitating institution and received incentive. The service provider received an incentive of Rs 20 (Rs 10 for assembling and Rs 10 for distribution for each light) and the distributor received Rs 30 for each lamp they repair. The service providers also trained the teachers on how to operate the lamps.

Teachers were trained on the operation of the product, they collected the amount from the students and provided the lamps to the students. They gave the amount received and student information to the implementing agency. School going children are the ultimate users of the solar urja lamps. They received the lamps from the teachers at subsidised rate. They used these lamps during evening hours for study purpose.

12.2 Recommendations

Use of Non-Governmental Organizations (NGOs), Cooperatives, and Self-Help Groups (SHGs) as a Distribution Channel for Clean Energy Products in Rural Areas: Manufacturers are finding it challenging to gain access to rural places in order to implement sustainable energy goods. They become reluctant to establish a distribution network if they cannot guarantee a particular amount of sales volume to justify the initial expenditure. Manufacturers must embrace sustainable energy goods in rural regions by integrating individuals from local NGOs, cooperatives, and SHGs in order to develop the distribution network. NGOs, cooperatives, and SHGs have a significant effect in rural regions since they focus on sustainable development by offering avenues for income generating. As a result, producers must collaborate with NGOs, cooperatives, and SHGs to spread sustainable energy goods in rural regions. Manufacturers must include them in their distribution channels in order to ensure last-mile delivery of sustainable energy products or services in rural regions. They must make use of the available infrastructure and build grassroots networking. They must educate and inform people about the benefits of adopting clean energy goods over unclean products, as well as the utilisation of clean energy products for revenue production. These initiatives will eventually aid in the spread of clean energy products in rural regions.

Members of NGOs, cooperatives, and SHGs must participate in decision-making. They must be involved in the price and margin determination of renewable energy products. Manufacturers must give them with technical and administrative training in order for clean energy goods to be distributed in rural regions. Members of NGOs, cooperatives, and SHGs can become selling agents for manufacturers, wholesalers, rural retailers, and so on.

Manufacturers must implement an incentive-based compensation system for generating client leads and timely service delivery by members of NGOs, cooperatives, and SHGs, which will aid in the spread of sustainable energy goods in rural regions.

Members of NGOs, cooperatives, and SHGs can approach manufacturers directly to acquire and sell the company's goods to rural customers since they are in direct contact with the rural consumers. This will instil a sense of entrepreneurial growth in them, assisting them in expanding their revenue. Manufacturers, on the other hand, will receive feedback on their sold products, learn the consumers' individual requirements and desires, and set about producing relevant iterations that will aid in the proliferation of clean energy items in rural regions.

Use of Rural Centric Models for Diffusion of Clean Energy Products in Rural Areas: Clean energy products need to be available through various rural centric models. Clean energy products available through haats, village malls, petrol pumps, through associated distribution and rural innovation centres will help in diffusion of clean energy products in rural areas. Other possible distribution partners can be post offices, photocopy shops, electrical shops, kirana stores, local tiffin stalls, etc. present in the local area. This will help in diffusion of clean energy products in rural areas.

Promotional Activities for Diffusion of Clean Energy Products in Rural Areas: For promotion of clean energy products in rural areas various promotional activities can be undertaken. Creating awareness programs by conducting live demonstration of the clean energy products in local language, using visual, pictorial advertisements of clean energy product, conducting door-to-door campaign, conducting cycle rally, participating in rural melas, trade fairs, exhibitions, conducting road shows, performing street plays, campaigning through auto-rickshaws by using loud speakers for communication purpose, conducting puppet shows, showing documentary films, etc. are some of the strategies which can be undertaken for diffusion of clean energy products in rural areas.

Collaborative Approach for Diffusion of Clean Energy Products in Rural Areas: For diffusion of clean energy products in rural areas, a collaborative approach among facilitating institutions, implementing agencies, financing institutions and other actors needs to be focused. Collaborative approach can be undertaken through technical collaboration, marketing collaboration, financial and consulting collaboration.

In technical collaboration, the manufacturers need to provide clean energy products, technical know-hows, trainings and services to the facilitating institutions and implementing agencies. In marketing collaboration, manufacturers, corporate houses, etc. need to agree to adopt the clean energy product though NGOs, cooperatives and SHGs present in the local area. They should be their channel partners for selling and distribution of clean energy products in rural areas. In financial collaboration, government, banks, donors, corporate houses, etc. need to agree to provide capital, financial assistance to the facilitating institution and the implementing agency for diffusion of clean energy products in the rural areas. In consulting collaboration, the facilitating institution, implementing agencies, etc. need to collaborate with each other for mentoring, providing guidance and seek support services for diffusion of clean energy products in the rural areas. They also need to exchange knowledge, skill, information, etc. among each other for diffusion of clean energy products in rural areas.

Use of Local Resources for Diffusion of Clean Energy Products in Rural Areas: Manufacturers do have access to the rural areas, but they find it difficult to sale their products in the rural areas due to varied reasons, starting from understanding the perception of the consumers whether to buy the product, price of the product, place of its availability to promotion of the product. The possible approach to overcome this problem is to use the local resources available in the region. Use of local resources basically focuses on involving local people, youths of the village, local shop owners, etc. of local area. Use of clean energy products for local value addition need to be focused. This will help in diffusion of clean energy products in rural areas.

Product-Bundling Strategy and Product-Sharing Strategy: Here the clean energy products need to be offered in a comprehensive package in a low price. For example, a solar operated drip irrigation system accompanied with sprinklers is a product-bundling strategy. Product-sharing strategy can be a self-managed instalment scheme, where a group of farmers can come together to buy the solar operated drip irrigation system and use it through a lottery system. This process can be repeated every month till all the farmers get the chance of using the system. This scheme is easy, interest free, self-managed and can become popular among the rural consumers. This will help in diffusion of clean energy products in rural areas.

Formation of JGLs for Diffusion of Clean Energy Products in Rural Areas: Where there is no feasibility of inclusion of NGOs, cooperatives and SHGs for undertaking diffusion of clean energy products, then formation of Joint Liability Groups (JLGs) can be undertaken for taking group loans in rural areas, which can help in the diffusion of clean energy products in rural areas. Five to eight members can be mobilised for formation of a JLG, who can apply for group loans. There are some reasons for forming JLGs instead of seeking individual loans. Firstly, the branch of the bank will be under pressure for processing individual loans applications and it will be time consuming. Secondly, JLGs automatically could create peer pressure for everyone within the group to pay their share every month. Third, instead of each member going to the bank every month, the members can share that responsibility among each other. Finally, when the members have more income in certain seasons, they can have the option of depositing more money in their JLG accounts, in order to save up for the times when their incomes might be low. Here the branch manager of the bank needs to be instrumental in facilitating the loans and should be keen on financing more innovative livelihood initiatives. With getting of loans, the members can procure clean energy products, spare parts, etc. from the producer directly, which will be sold to rural consumers to earn revenue. With the cash collected from the rural consumers, a member can go on procuring more clean energy products and get into a healthy cycle of buying and selling process. Eventually, once the business is well established, the loan needs to paid back with the interest amount to the bank. This will help in diffusion of clean energy products in rural areas.

Product Rent Model: The product rent model needs to be undertaken when the rural consumers cannot afford high priced clean energy product. They can rent the product to other consumers for a specific amount and period of time. This model will help in generating income for the rural consumer, easy repayment of loans and enhancing quality of life. Demonstration and creating awareness on the benefits of using clean energy products needs to be undertaken among the rural consumers for diffusion of the product. Raising awareness among the bankers, lenders, donors, other private sectors institutions pursuing international agreement and commitment to achieve the goal of universal access to clean energy also needs to be undertaken for achieving diffusion of clean energy products in the rural areas.

All the above recommendations will help diffusion of clean energy products in rural areas.

References

- Abu-Aligah, M. (2011). Design of Photovoltaic Water Pumping System and Compare it with Diesel Powered Pump. Jordan Journal of Mechanical & Industrial Engineering, 5(3), pp. 273–280.
- Adite, C. (1996). Haats and Melas, Business Today, October 7-21, pp. 125-133.
- Adurodija, F., Asia, I., & Chendo, M. (1998). The Market Potential of Photovoltaic Systems In Nigeria. Solar Energy, 64(4-6), pp. 133–139.
- Afzaal Ali, I. A. (2012). Environment Friendly Products: Factors that Influence the Green Purchase Intentions of Pakistani Consumers. Pak Journal of Eng. Technol. Sci. , 2 (1), 84-117.
- Agoramoorthy, G., & Hsu, M. J. (2009). Lighting the Lives of the Impoverished in India's Rural and Tribal Drylands. Human Ecology, 37(4), pp. 513–517.
- Al-Smairan, M. (2012). Application of photovoltaic array for pumping water as an alternative to diesel engines in Jordan Badia, Tall Hassan station: Case study. Renewable and Sustainable Energy Reviews, 16(7), pp. 4500–4507.
- Ali, A., Khan, A. & Ahmed, I. (2011). Determinants of Pakistani Consumers Green Purchase Behaviour: Some Insight from A Developing Country. International Journal of Business and Social Science, 2, pp. 217 - 226.
- Anderson, T., Curtis. A., and C. Wittig. (2015). Definition and Theory in Social Innovation: The Theory of Social Innovation and International Approaches. ZSI Discussion Paper, Nr. 33, Zentrum für Soziale

Innovation, Wien, Austria.

- A, Prakash. (2000). Responsible Care: An Assessment, Business & Society, Vol. 39, N0. 2; pp. 618-637.
- Arcury A. Thomas. Environmental Attitude and Environmental Knowledge. Human Organization, Volume 49, Number 4, Winter 1990, pp. 300-304.
- Aryal, K. P., Chaudhary, P., Pandit, S. & Sharma, G. (2009). Consumer's Willingness to Pay for Organic Products: A Case from Kathmandu Valley. The Journal of Agriculture and Environment, 10, pp. 12 - 22.
- Arrow, K. J. (1962). Economic Welfare and the Allocation of Resources for Invention. The Rate and Direction of Inventive Activity, pp. 609–626.
- Ajzen, I. (1991). The theory of planned behavior. Organizational Behavior and Human Decision Processes, 50(2), pp. 179–211.
- Akinboro, F., & Adejumobi, L. A. (2012). Solar Energy Installation in Nigeria: Observations, Prospect, Problems, and Solution. Transnational Journal of Science and Technology, 2(4), pp. 73-84.
- Akranaviciute, D., and Ruzevicius, J. (2007). Quality of life and its components' measurement. Engineering Economics,2 , pp. 43-48.
- Akunne, A. F., Louis, V. R., Sanon, M., & Sauerborn, R. (2006). Biomass solid fuel and acute respiratory infections: The ventilation factor. International Journal of Hygiene and Environmental Health, 209(5), pp. 445–450.
- Bairiganjan, S., and S. Sanyal. (2013). The last 50 mile: Using LVE Networks for increasing Clean Energy Access. New Ventures India, Hyderabad.

REFERENCES

- Barendregt, B. and Jaffe, R. (2014). The Paradoxes of Eco-Chic. Green consumption: the global rise of eco-chic, Bloomsbury Publishing house. pp 1-16.
- Balakrishnan, K., Sambandam, S., Ramaswamy, P., Mehta, S., & Smith, K. R. (2004). Exposure assessment for respirable particulates associated with household fuel use in rural districts of Andhra Pradesh, India. Journal of Exposure Science & Environmental Epidemiology, 14(S1).
- Battisti, G., & Stoneman, P. (1998). The Diffusion of Unleaded Petrol: An Anglo-Italian Comparison. Labour, 12(2), pp. 255–278.
- Baker, L., Wagner, T. H., Singer, S., & Bundorf, M. K. (2003). Use of the Internet and E-mail for Health Care Information. Jama, 289(18), pp. 2400.
- Banerjee, G., Barnes, F. D., Singh, B., Mayer, K., Samad, H. & Narayan, B. (2014). Power for all: electricity access challenge in India. Retrieved from http://documents.worldbank.org/curated/en/ 562191468041399641/Power-for-all-electricity-access-challenge-in-India
- Barron, M., & Torero, M. (2017). Household electrification and indoor air pollution. Journal of Environmental Economics and Management, 86, pp. 81–92.
- Baquié, S., & Urpelainen, J. (2017). Access to modern fuels and satisfaction with cooking arrangements: Survey evidence from rural India. Energy for Sustainable Development, 38, pp. 34–47.
- Berth, N. (2011). The Importance of Being Seen to be Green - An Empirical Investigation of Green Marketing Strategies in Business-to-Business Organizations. Australia: Auckland University of Technology.

- Berger, W. (2001). Catalysts for the diffusion of photovoltaics? A review of selected programmes. Progress in Photovoltaics: Research and Applications, 9(2), pp. 145–160.
- Berghman, L., Matthyssens, P., & Vandenbempt, K. (2006). Building competences for new customer value creation: An exploratory study. Industrial Marketing Management, 35(8), pp. 961–973.
- Bhushan, C., and Kumar, J. (2012). Going Remote: Re-inventing the off-grid solar revolution for clean energy for all. Centre for Science and Environment, New Delhi. Retrieved from https: // www. worldcat. Org / title/ going-remote-re-inventing-the-off-grid-solar-revolution-for-clean-energy-for-all/oclc/892961343
- Bloom, D. E., Craig, P. H., & Malaney, P. N. (2001). The quality of life in rural Asia. Oxford: Oxford University Press.
- Borden, N. H. (1984). The Concept of Marketing Mix. Journal of Advertising Research, 1(9), pp. 2-7.
- Boztepe, A. (2012). Green Marketing and its impact on Consumer Behaviour. Europe Journal of Economics and Political Studies, Ejeps-5(1), 5-21.
- Brown, L. A. (1981). Innovation diffusion: a new perspective. London: Methuen.
- Brown J., Bowling, A., and Flynn, T. (2004). Models of quality of life: a taxonomy and systematic review of the literature, University of Sheffield, FORUM project. Retrieved from http://www.shef.ac.uk/ageingresearch.
- BP Statistical Review of World Energy, 2016. Retrieved from http://large.stanford.edu courses/2017/ph241/burke1/docs/bp_2016.pdf
- BP Statistical Review of World Energy, 2019. Retrieved from https:// www. bp. com/ content/dam/bp/

businesssites/en/global/corporate/pdfs/ energyeconomics/statistical-review/bp-stats-review-2019-full-report.pdf

- Bozeman, B. (2000). Technology transfer and public policy: a review of research and theory. Research Policy, 29(4-5), pp. 627–655.
- Burgelman, R. A., Christensen, C. M., & Wheelwright, S. C. (2009). Strategic management of technology and innovation. New York: McGraw-Hill Higher Education.
- Cabraal, R. A., Barnes, D. F., & Agarwal, S. G. (2005). Productive Uses Of Energy For Rural Development. Annual Review of Environment and Resources, 30 (1), pp. 117–144.
- Caird, S., Roy, R., & Herring, H. (2008). Improving the energy performance of UK households: Results from surveys of consumer adoption and use of low- and zero-carbon technologies. Energy Efficiency, 1(2), pp. 149–166.
- Candan, B. &Yildirim, S., 2013. Investigating the Relationship between Consumption Values and Personal Values of Green Product Buyers. International Journal of Economics and Management Sciences, 2(12), pp. 29-40.
- Chang, C. (2011). Feeling ambivalent about going green – Implication For Green Advertising Processing. Journal of Advertising, 40(4), 19-31.
- Charter, M. &Polonsky, M. J., 1999. Greener Marketing: A Global Perspective on Greening Marketing Practice. 2nd Edition.
- Chase, D. & Smith, T. K. (1992). Consumer Keen on Green but Marketers Don't Deliver. Advertising Age, 63, pp. 82 - 84. Coddington, W. (1993). Environmental Marketing: Positive Strategies for Reaching the Green

Consumer, New York, United States: McGraw-Hill Inc.

- Cherian, J. et al. (2012). Green Marketing: A Study of Consumers' Attitude towards Environment Friendly Products. Asian Social Science, Vol. 8 Issue 12, p.117.

- Crane, A. (2000), Facing the Backlash, Green Market and Strategic Reorientation in the 1990s. Journal of Strategic Marketing, 8, pp. 277 - 296.

- Deli-G., Gillpatrick Z., T., Marusic, M., Pantelic, D. &Kuruvilla, S.J (2011). Hedonic and Functional Shopping Values and Everyday Product Purchase: Findings from the Indian Study. International Journal of Business Insights &Transformation, 4(1), 65-72.

- Diamantopoulos, A., Schlegelmilch, B.B., Sinkovics R. and Bohlen,G. M. (2003), Can socio-demographics still play a role in profiling green consumers? A review of the evidence and an empirical investigation, Journal of Business Research, 56, (6), 465-480.

- Dimitrova, B. (2005). Carr A J, Higginson I J, Robinson P G, (editors). Quality of life. London: BMJ Books, 2003. 133 pp. ISBN 0-7279-1544-4. European Journal of Public Health, 15(6), pp. 668–668.

- Caselli, F., & Coleman, W. J. (2001). Cross-Country Technology Diffusion: The Case of Computers. American Economic Review, 91(2), pp. 328–335.

- CEA (2017): Installed Capacity March 2017, Central Electricity Authority, New Delhi. (n.d.). Retrieved from http:// www. cea.nic.in/ reports/ monthly/ installed capacity/2017/installed_capacity-10.pdf

- Census of India. (2011). Office of the Registrar General and Census Commissioner, India, New Delhi. 2011.

- Central Pollution Control Board, (CPCB) (2010). Status of Vehicular Pollution Control Programme in India, pp. 2-6.

- Chakravorty, U., Emerick, K., & Ravago, M.-L. (2016). Lighting Up the Last Mile: The Benefits and Costs of Extending Electricity to the Rural Poor. SSRN Electronic Journal.
- Chambers, R., & Conway, G. (1992). Sustainable rural livelihoods: practical concepts for the 21st century. Brighton: Institute of Development Studies.
- Chandel, S., Naik, M. N., & Chandel, R. (2015). Review of solar photovoltaic water pumping system technology for irrigation and community drinking water supplies. Renewable and Sustainable Energy Reviews, 49, pp. 1084–1099.
- Chetan, S.S., et.al. (2016). Concurrent Evaluation Report of Million SoUL Program in India. Indian Institute of Technology. Bombay.
- Chetan, S.S. (2018). Dawn of Solar PV Cooking. Akshay Urja. pp. 22-26.
- Chilcott, R.P. (2006). Compendium of chemical hazards: diesel. Chemical Hazards and Poisons Division (HQ). UK Health Protection Agency (HPA), Oxfordshire.
- Christopher Gan, H. Y.-H. (2008). Consumers' purchasing behavior towards green products in New. Innovative Marketing , 4 (1).
- Caird, S., & Roy, R. (2008). User-Centred Improvements to Energy Efficiency Products And Renewable Energy Systems: Research On Household Adoption And Use. International Journal of Innovation Management, 12(03), pp. 327–355.
- Clean Edge: $246B Market for Solar, Wind, Biofuels in 2011 ... (n.d.). Retrieved from https://www.greentechmedia.com/articles/read/clean-edge-246b-market-for-solar-wind-biofuels-

in-2011

- Cutler, D., & Mcclellan, M. (1996). The Determinants of Technological Change in Heart Attack Treatment.
- Davis, F. D. (1989). Perceived Usefulness, Perceived Ease of Use, and User Acceptance of Information Technology. MIS Quarterly, 13(3), pp. 319.
- Das, B. (2015). Diffusion of Information and Communication Technology: Evidence from Indian Agriculture. Unpublished Ph.D Thesis, Centre for Development Studies, JNU.
- Das, S.S., & Panda, H. (2017). Smokeless chulha – A way for enhancing quality of life. International Journal of Research and Scientific Innovation,4, pp. 70–78. Retrieved from https://www.rsisinternational.org/IJRSI/Issue44/70-78.pdf
- Deutschmann, P. J., & Danielson, W. A. (1960). Diffusion of Knowledge of the Major News Story. Journalism Quarterly, 37(3), pp. 345–355.
- Dholakia, U. M., Bagozzi, R. P., & Pearo, L. K. (2004). A social influence model of consumer participation in network- and small-group-based virtual communities. International Journal of Research in Marketing, 21(3), pp. 241–263.
- Dholakia, R. R., & Kshetri, N. (2004). Factors Impacting the Adoption of the Internet among SMEs. Small Business Economics, 23(4), pp. 311–322.
- Diener, E., Suh, E. M., Lucas, R. E., & Smith, H. L. (1999). Subjective well-being: Three decades of progress. Psychological Bulletin, 125(2), pp. 276–302.
- Dinkelman, T. (2011). The Effects of Rural Electrification on Employment: New Evidence from South Africa. American Economic Review, 101(7), pp. 3078–3108.

- Dishna. S., Elmar. D., and Bandlamudi G. C. (2005). Lighting technologies. Retrieved from http://www.uni-oldenburg. de/ ppre/ download/ Downloads/ Lighting_Technologies_1.pdf.
- Durrani, B.A., Godil, D.I., Baig, M.U and Sajid, S. (2015). Impact of Brand Image on Buying Behaviour Among Teenagers. European Scientific Journal, 11 (51), pp. 155-168.
- Dutt, G. S. (1994). Illumination and sustainable development. Part I: Technology and economics. Energy for Sustainable Development, 1(1), pp. 23–35.
- Draper, N. R. & Smith, H., 1998. Applied Regression Analysis. Third Edition ed. s.l. Wiley-Interscience.
- Drinkwater, M., and McEwan, M. (1992). Household food security and environmental sustainability in farming systems research: developing sustainable livelihoods. Paper presented to the Adaptive Planning Research Team Bi-annual Review Meeting, Mangu, Zambia, 13-16 April.
- Essam E. Aboul Zahaba, Aziza M.Zakib and Mohamed M.EI-SotouhyDesign and control of a Standalone PV water pumping system. Journal of Electrical system and Information Technology, 2017, pp.322-337.
- Ecosystem approach vital for clean energy access: WWF-India & SELCO. (n.d.). Retrieved from http://www.wwfindia.org/?14861/Ecosystem-approach-vital-for-clean-energy-access-WWF-India--SELCO
- Energizing India. A Joint Report published by NITI Aayog and IEEJ, (2017). Retrieved from https:// niti.gov.in/ writereaddata/ files/ document_publication/ Energy Booklet.pdf.

- Engel, J. F., Blackwell, R. D., & Miniard, P. W. (1993). Consumer behaviour. Fort Worth, TX: Dryden Press.
- Engerbretson, M., 2013. Cosmetics Testing on Animals in the Spotlight at Jakarta Fashion Week: ASEAN Takes Notice. The Huffington Post, 29 (10).
- Environmental Awareness and the Changing Attitude of the Students and the Public in Coimbatore towards Green Products. Research Journal of Social Science and Management, 1, pp. 75 - 84.
- Fabrigar, L. R., MacCallum, R. C., Wegener, D. T. &Strahan, E. J., 1999. Evaluating the Use of Exploratory Factor Analysis in Psychological Research. Psychological Methods, 4(No.3), pp. 272-299.
- Faith, D.O., & Agwu, M.E. (2014). A review of the Effect of Pricing Strategies on the Purchase of Consumer Goods. International Journal of Research in Management, Science & Technology, 2 (2), pp. 88-102.
- Ferrell, O. C., & Hartline, M. D. (2005). Marketing strategy. Mason, OH: Thomson South-Western.
- Fichman, R. G. (2000). The Diffusion and Assimilation of Information Technology Innovations, in R. W. Zmud (Ed.), Framing The Domains of IT Management: Projecting the Future Through the Past, Cincinnati, OH: Pinnaflex Press, pp. 105-128.
- Flanagan, J. C. (1978). A research approach to improving our quality of life. American Psychologist, 33(2), pp. 138–147.
- Fronseca-Santos, B., Corrêa, M. A. & Chorilli, M., 2015. Sustainability, Natural and Organic Cosmetics: Consumer, Products, Eficacy, Toxicological and Regulatory Considerations. Brazilian Joural of Pharmaceutical Sciences, Jan/Mar, 51(1), pp. 17-26.

- G. Palanikumar, S. Shanmugan, ChithambaramVengatesanand Periyasami Selvaraju, "Evaluation of fuzzy inference in box type solar cooking food image of thermal effect", Environmental and Sustainability Indicators, vol.1-2, (2019), pp.1-10.
- Garber, L. L., & Dotson, M. J. (2002). A method for the selection of appropriate business-to-business integrated marketing communications mixes. Journal of Marketing Communications, 8(1), pp. 1–17.
- Garg, R. (2014). Free Solar Lanterns to Below Poverty Line Girls in India: A Step Toward Achieving Millennium Development Goals. Social Work in Public Health, 29(3), pp. 189–195.
- Gebreegziabher, Z., Mekonnen, A., Kassie, M., & Köhlin, G. (2012). Urban energy transition and technology adoption: The case of Tigrai, northern Ethiopia. Energy Economics, 34(2), pp. 410–418.
- Georgopoulos, B. S. (1967). James S. Coleman, Elihu Katz, and Herbert Menzel. Medical innovation: A diffusion study. Indianapolis: The Bobbs-Merrill Company, 1966. Behavioral Science, 12(6), pp. 481–483.
- Ghoshal, S., & Bartlett, C. A. (1988). Creation, Adoption and Diffusion of Innovations by Subsidiaries of Multinational Corporations. Journal of International Business Studies, 19(3), pp. 365–388.
- Gilgeous, V. (1998). Manufacturing managers: their quality of working life. Integrated Manufacturing Systems, 9(3), pp. 173–181.
- Global Energy Transition A Roadmap to 2050. (n.d.). Retrieved from https://www.irena.org/publications/2018/Apr/Global-Energy-Transition-A-Roadmap-to-2050

- Gordon, S. B., Bruce, N. G., Grigg, J., Hibberd, P. L., Kurmi, O. P., Lam, K.-B. H., Martin, W. J. (2014). Respiratory risks from household air pollution in low and middle income countries. The Lancet Respiratory Medicine, 2(10), pp. 823–860.
- Gould, C. F., & Urpelainen, J. (2018). LPG as a clean cooking fuel: Adoption, use, and impact in rural India. Energy Policy, 122, pp. 395–408.
- Government of India. The Electricity Act, 2003. New Delhi: The Gazette of India; 2003 [Extraordinary, 2003]
- Greenhalgh, T., Robert, G., Macfarlane, F., Bate, P., & Kyriakidou, O. (2004). Diffusion of Innovations in Service Organizations: Systematic Review and Recommendations. The Milbank Quarterly, 82(4), pp. 581–629.
- Gross, R., Leach, M., & Bauen, A. (2003). Progress in renewable energy. Environment International, 29(1), pp. 105–122.
- Haas, B. K. (1999). Clarification and Integration of Similar Quality of Life Concepts. Image: the Journal of Nursing Scholarship, 31(3), pp. 215–220.
- Hailes, J., 2007. The New Green Consumer Guide. London: Simon & Schuster.
- Hannan, M. T., & Freeman, J. (1989). Organizational ecology. Cambridge, MA: Harvard University Press.
- Hasan, J., Hartoyo, H., Sumarwan, U., & Suharjo, B. (2012). Factors Analysis in Desire to Buy Environmental Friendly Products - Case Study for Air Condition Products. International Business Research, 5(8).
- Harshit Jain,Nikunj Gangrade, Sumit Paul, Harshal Gangrade, Jishnu Ghosh, "Design and fabrication of solar pesticide sprayer", IJARIIE, 4(2018), P.1715-1727.

- Heltberg, R. (2004). Fuel switching: evidence from eight developing countries. Energy Economics, 26(5), pp. 869–887.
- Helper, S., and M. Sako. (1995). Supplier Relations in Japan and the United States: Are They Converging? Sloan Management Review, Spring, pp. 77–84.
- Hilario Terres, Arturo Lizardi, Raymundo López, Mabel Vaca and Sandra Chávez, "Mathematical Model to Study Solar Cookers Box-Type with Internal Reflectors", Energy Procedia, Vol.57 (2014), pp. 1583 – 1592.
- Hoerup, S.L. (2001). Diffusion of an innovation: computer technology integration and the role of collaboration. Doctoral dissertation, Virginia Polytechnic Institute and State University, ProQuest Digital Dissertations. (UMI No.AAT 3031436).
- Holtorf, H., Urmee, T., Calais, M., & Pryor, T. (2015). A model to evaluate the success of Solar Home Systems. Renewable and Sustainable Energy Reviews, 50, pp. 245–255.
- Hubbard, T. N. (2000). The Demand for Monitoring Technologies: The Case of Trucking. The Quarterly Journal of Economics, 115(2), pp. 533–560.
- Hughes, B. (1990). Quality of life. In: Peace. SM (ed), Researching social gerontology. London. Sage Publications.
- Human Development Reports. (n.d.). Retrieved from http://hdr.undp.org/en/2018-MPI
- IEA (2013). World Energy Outlook. International Energy Agency (IEA), Paris.
- Igbaria, M. (1993). User acceptance of microcomputer technology: An empirical test. Omega, 21(1), pp. 73–90.
- Indian Petroleum and Natural Gas Statistics (2017), MoPNG Economic and Statistics Division, (2017), pp.

57.

- Islam, S. & ZabinI. (2003). Consumer's attitude towards purchasing of green food. European Journal of Business and Management, Vol. 5, p.no.9, 2222-2839.
- Jacobson, Arne, Bond, C., T., Lam, Hultman, & Nathan. (2013). Black Carbon and Kerosene Lighting: An Opportunity for Rapid Action on Climate Change and Clean Energy for Development. Retrieved from https:// www. osti. gov/ servlets /purl/22110332
- Jacobsson, S. (2004). Transforming the energy sector: the evolution of technological systems in renewable energy technology. Industrial and Corporate Change, 13(5), pp. 815–849.
- Jacobs, S. J., & Herselman, M. (2006). Information Access for Development: A Case Study at a Rural Community Centre in South Africa. Issues in Informing Science and Information Technology, 3, pp. 295–306.
- Jain, A., Choudhury, P., and K. Ganesan. (2015). Clean, Affordable and Sustainable Cooking Energy for India: Possibilities and Realities beyond LPG. Retrieved from https:// www. ceew. in/sites/ default/ files/ CEEW-Clean-affordable-and-sustainable- cooking-energy-in-India-Feb2015.pdf
- Janse, A., Gemke, R., Uiterwaal, C., Tweel, I. V. D., Kimpen, J., & Sinnema, G. (2004). Quality of life: patients and doctors dont always agree: a meta-analysis. Journal of Clinical Epidemiology, 57(7), pp. 653–661.
- Jetter, J., Zhao, Y., Smith, K. R., Khan, B., Yelverton, T., Decarlo, P., & Hays, M. D. (2012). Pollutant Emissions and Energy Efficiency under Controlled Conditions for Household Biomass Cookstoves and Implications for Metrics Useful in Setting International Test Standards. Environmental Science & Technology, 46(19), pp.

10827–10834.

- Joonas Rokka, L. U. (2008). Preference for green packaging in consumer product choices – Do consumers care? International Journal of Consumer Studies , pp. 516–525.
- Joshua Folaranmi, "Performance Evaluation of a Double-Glazed Box-Type Solar Oven with Reflector", Journal of Renewable Energy, 2013, pp.1-8.
- Jurate Banyte, L. B. (2010). Ivestigation of Green Consumer Profile: A Case Of Lithuanian Market of Eco Friendly Food Products. Economics And Management , pp. 374-383.
- Kalotra, A. (2013). Rural Marketing Potential in India-An Analytical Study. International Journal of Advanced Research in Computer Science and Software Engineering, 3(1), pp. 1-10.
- Kaman, L. (2008). Opportunities for green marketing: young consumers. Marketing Intelligence & Planning, 26, pp. 573-586.
- Kashyap, P. Rural Marketing. 2nd Edition, Dorling Kindersey (India) Pvt Ltd., Pearson, New Delhi, (2012).
- Katsikeas, C. S., & Al-Khalifa, A. (1993). The issue of import motivation in manufacturer—overseas distributor relationships: Implications for exporters. Journal of Marketing Management, 9(1), pp. 65–77.
- Kauffman, R. J., Mcandrews, J., & Wang, Y.-M. (2000). Opening the "Black Box" of Network Externalities in Network Adoption. Information Systems Research, 11(1), pp. 61–82.
- Kabiru, S. A. (2016). Socio-Economic Infrastructure and National Development: An Analytical Assessment from Nigerian Perspective. IOSR Journal of Humanities and Social Science, 21(10), pp. 40–46.

- Khandoker Mahmudur Rahman, M. H. (2011). Exploring Price Sensitivity of a Green Brand: A Consumers' Perspective. World Review of Business Research , 1 (2), pp. 84 - 97.
- Kolhe M, Joshi J.C, and Kothari D. P. Performance Analysis of a Direct Coupled Photovoltaic Water-Pumping system. IEEE Transactions on Energy Conversion, 2004, pp.613-618.
- Kotler, P. (1999). Marketing management: the Millennium Edition. Upper Saddle River, NJ: Prentice Hall.
- Kotler, P., G.Armstrong, V. Wong., and J. Saunders. (2008). Principles of Marketing. Prentice Hall.
- Kotler, P., and Keller, K.L. (2016). Marketing Management. New Jersey: Pearson Prentice Hall.
- Kennickell, A. B., & Kwast, M. L. (1997). Who Uses Electronic Banking? Results from the 1995 Survey of Consumer Finances. Finance and Economics Discussion Series, 1997(35), pp. 1–48.
- Kumar, V., Kumar, U., & Persaud, A. (1999). The Journal of Technology Transfer, 24(1), pp. 81–96.
- Kumar, S. (2011). Analyzing the Factors Affecting Consumer Awareness on Organic Foods in India, Paper presented at 21st Annual IFAMA World Forum and Symposium on the Road to 2050: Sustainability as a Business Opportunity, Frankfurt, Germany during June 20-23, 2011.
- Kweka, A. E., Massawe, F. A., Wambura, S., & Mignouna, D. (2011). Feasibility Study on Solar Electrification for Poverty Alleviation in Rural Communities in Southern Tanzania. Proceedings of the ISES Solar World Congress 2011, pp. 80–92.

- Kwon, H. S., & Chidambaram, L. (2000). A test of the technology acceptance model: the case of cellular telephone adoption. Proceedings of the 33rd Annual Hawaii International Conference on System Sciences.
- Lan, P., & Young, S. (1996). International technology transfer examined at technology component level: a case study in China. Technovation, 16(6), pp. 277–286.
- Lay, J., Ondraczek, J., & Stoever, J. (2013). Renewables in the energy transition: Evidence on solar home systems and lighting fuel choice in Kenya. Energy Economics, 40, pp. 350–359.
- Leach, G. (1992), The Energy Transition, Energy Policy, 20, (2), pp. 116–123.
- Lehmann, D. R., & Oshaughnessy, J. (1974). Difference in Attribute Importance for Different Industrial Products. Journal of Marketing, 38(2), pp. 36–42.
- Lin, B.-W. (2003). Technology transfer as technological learning: a source of competitive advantage for firms with limited R&D resources. R And D Management, 33(3), pp. 327–341.
- Lin, N.H. (2007). The Effect of Brand Image and Product Knowledge on Purchase Intention Moderated by Price Discount. Journal of International Management Studies,8, pp. 121-132.
- Lipscomb, M., Mobarak, A. M., & Barham, T. (2013). Development Effects of Electrification: Evidence from the Topographic Placement of Hydropower Plants in Brazil. American Economic Journal: Applied Economics, 5(2), pp. 200 231.
- Lovell, S. A. (1998). Technology Transfer: Testing a Theoretical Model of the Human, Machine, Mission and Medium Components. Unpublished Msg. Thesis. Cranfield: College of Aeronautics, Cranfield University.

- Lovelock, C. H., Patterson, P., & Walker, R. H. (2004). Services marketing: an Asia-Pacific and Australian perspective. Frenchs Forest, NSW: Prentice Hall.

- Luis Bernardo LópezSosaa, Mauricio González Avilésa, Dante González Péreza and YuritziSolísGutiérreza, "Rural Solar Cookers, an alternative to reduce the timber resource extraction through the use of renewable energy sources: technology transfer and monitoring project", Energy Procedia, vol. 57 (2014) 1593 – 1602.

- Luthra, S., Kumar, S., Garg, D., & Haleem, A. (2015). Barriers to renewable / sustainable energy technologies adoption: Indian perspective. Renewable and Sustainable Energy Reviews, 41, pp. 762–776.

- M. Balakrishnan, A. Claude and D. R. Arun Kumar, "Engineering, design and fabrication of a solar cooker with parabolic concentrator for heating, drying and cooking purposes", Archives of Applied Science Research, vol.4,(2012), pp. 1636-1649.

- Mahapatra, S., Chanakya, H., & Dasappa, S. (2009). Evaluation of various energy devices for domestic lighting in India: Technology, economics and CO2 emissions. Energy for Sustainable Development, 13(4), pp. 271–279.

- Maheshwari, A. &Malhotra, G. (2011). Green Marketing: A Study on Indian Youth. International Journal of Management and Strategy, 2, pp. 1 - 15.

- Mannarswamy, S. (2011). A Study of Environmental Awareness and the Changing Attitude of the Students and the Public in Coimbatore towards Green Products. Research Journal of Social Science and Management, 1, pp. 75 – 84.

- Maranville, S. (1992). Entrepreneurship in the Business Curriculum. Journal of Education for Business, 68(1), pp. 27–31.
- Martinot, E., & Cabraal, A. (2000). World Bank Solar Home Systems Projects. World Renewable Energy Congress VI, pp. 749–754.
- Mathur, K., Oliver, S., & Tripney, J. (2015). PROTOCOL: Access to Electricity for Improving Health, Education and Welfare in Low- and Middle-Income Countries: A Systematic Review. Campbell Systematic Reviews, 11(1), pp. 1–55.
- MacKenzie, D. A., & Wajcman, J. (1999). The social shaping of technology: how the refrigerator got its hum. Milton Keynes: Open University Press.
- Mavuri, S. (2011). Impact of Education and Income on Awareness Creation and Buying Decision in case of Solar Products in Visakhapatnam, India. World Journal of Social Sciences, 1(1), pp. 49- 68.
- McCarthy, E. J. (1964). Basic Marketing, A Managerial Approach. Homewood, IL: R.D. Irwin.
- Mccall, S. (1975). Quality of life. Social Indicators Research, 2(2), pp. 229–248.
- Mendelow, A.L. Environmental Scanning- The Impact of the Stakeholder Concept, (1981).
- Mills E. (1999). Fuel-based light: large CO2 source. International Association of Energy-Efficient Lighting Newsletter, 8(23). Retrieved from http://www.iaeel. org/IAEEL/NEWSL/1999/tva1999/ ett299.html.
- MoP (2017). (n.d.). Retrieved from http://powermin.nic.in/en/content/power-sector-glance-all-india
- MoP (2017). Ujwal Bharat 3 Years, Achievements and Initiatives of Ministry of Power, Coal, New & Renewable

Energy, and Mines, Government of India, pp. 24.

- Murali, R., Malhotra, S., Palit, D., & Sasmal, K. (2015). Socio-technical assessment of solar photovoltaic systems implemented for rural electrification in selected villages of Sundarbans region of India. AIMS Energy, 3(4), pp. 612–634.
- Narale, E. P. D., Rathore, N. S., & Kothari, S. (2013). Study of solar PV water pumping system for irrigation of horticulture crops. International Journal of Engineering Science Invention, 2(12), pp. 54–60.
- NCAER (1992). Evaluation Survey of Household Biogas Plants set up during Seventh Five Year Plan. National Council for Applied Economic Research, New Delhi.
- Niehof, A., and L. Price. Rural Livelihood Systems: A Conceptual Framework. UPWARD Working Paper Series No. 5, (2001). WU-UPWARD, Wageningen
- Peter, R., Ramaseshan, B., & Nayar, C. (2002). Conceptual model for marketing solar based technology to developing countries. Renewable Energy, 25(4), pp. 511–524.
- Meyer, G. (2004). Diffusion Methodology: Time to Innovate? Journal of Health Communication, 9(sup1), pp. 59–69.
- Mohanty, S. (2013). Marketing Consumer Durables in Indian Rural Market. Srusti Management Review, 6(2), pp. 13-18.
- Moore, G. A. (1991). Crossing the chasm marketing and selling technology products to mainstream customers. New York, NY: Harper Business.
- Nakarado, G. L. (1996). A marketing orientation is the key to a sustainable energy future. Energy Policy, 24(2), pp. 187–193.

REFERENCES

- OSullivan, A., & Sheffrin, S. M. (2003). Prentice Hall economics: principles in action. Needham, MA: Prentice Hall.
- Oxford English Dictionary, 7th Edition, 115th impression, (2019). pp. 152, 325, 499 and 571.
- Panda, H. (1996). Technological Capability Assessment of a Firm in the Electricity Sector. PhD. Thesis, pp. 19.
- Painuly, J. (2001). Barriers to renewable energy penetration; a framework for analysis. Renewable Energy, 24(1), pp. 73–89.
- Park, S.Y. (2009). An Analysis of the Technology Acceptance Model in Understanding University Students' Behavioral Intention to Use e-Learning. Journal of Educational Technology & Society, 12(3), pp. 150-162.
- Patnaik, A. A Study on Impact of Demographic factors on Eco-friendly buying decision. Indian Journal of Environmental Protection, 40 (7), pp. 775-780.
- Pederson, H. C., & Sanders, H. C. (1966). The Cooperative Extension Service. Journal of Farm Economics, 48(3), pp. 771.
- Porter, M. E. (1985). Competitive advantage: creating and sustaining superior performance. New York, NY: Free Press.
- Peattie, K., & Belz, F.-M. (2010). Sustainability marketing — An innovative conception of marketing. Marketing Review St. Gallen, 27(5), pp. 8–15.
- Harris, L. (1973). Review of CATV—A History of Community Antenna Television, by Mary Alice Mayer Phillips. Performing Arts Review, 4(1-2), pp. 91–97.
- R. Joshua, V. Vasu and P. Vincent. "Solar Sprayer - An Agriculture Implement", International Journal of Sustainable Agriculture, 2(2010), pp.16-19.

- Ramanathan, M. (1993). Linking Banks and SHGs. Sri Lankan Experience- RURAL FINANCE, 10, pp. 11-20.
- Ranjbarian, B., Shaemi, A., & Jolodar, S. Y. E. (2011). Assessing the Effectiveness of Electric Conservation Advertisements in Isfahan Channel Television. International Business Research, 4(3).
- Ramana. P.V. (1991). Biogas Programme in India, 1(3), pp. 1-12.
- Rassega, V., T, O., & T, C. (2015). Social Networks and the Buying Behavior of the Consumer. Journal of Global Economics, 03(04).
- Reddy, S., & Painuly, J. (2004). Diffusion of renewable energy technologies—barriers and stakeholders' perspectives. Renewable Energy, 29(9), pp. 1431–1447.
- Reddy, N., & Zhao, L. (1990). International technology transfer: A review. Research Policy, 19(4), pp. 285–307.
- Renewable energy potentials in Nigeria Ijeoma Vincent-Akpu ... (n.d.). Retrieved from https://conferences.iaia.org/2012/pdf/uploadpapers/ Final papers review process/ Vincent-Akpu, Ijeoma. Renewable energy potentials in Nigeria.pdf
- Retrieved from the Report by Petroleum Planning and Analysis Cell, (PPAC), (2019). Ministry of Petroleum and Natural Gas.
- Rogers, E.M., and Shoemaker, F.F. Communication of Innovations: A Cross-Cultural Approach. New York: Free Press, (1971).
- ROGERS, E.M. Diffusion of Innovations. 5th Edition, New York, NY: Free Press., (1962), (1983), (1995), (2003).
- Rollins, T. (1993). Using The Innovation Adoption Diffusion Model To Target Educational Programming. Journal of Agricultural Education, 34(4), pp. 46–54.

- Rubab, S., & Kandpal, T. C. (1997). Resource-Technology Combinations for Domestic Lighting in Rural India: A Comparative Financial Evaluation. Energy Sources, 19(8),pp. 813–831.
- Ryan, B., and N. Gross. (1943). The Diffusion of Hybrid Seed Corn in Two Iowa Communities. Rural Sociology, (8), pp. 15-24.
- S.Charvani, K.Sowmya, M.Malathi , P.Rajani4, K.Saibaba"Design and fabrication of a solar sprayer", International Journal of science Technology and Management, 6(2017), pp.589-596.
- Saade, R., Nebebe, F., & Tan, W. (2007). Viability of the "Technology Acceptance Model" in Multimedia Learning Environments: A Comparative Study. Proceedings of the 2007 InSITE Conference.
- Saloner, G., & Shepard, A. (1995). Adoption of Technologies with Network Effects: An Empirical Examination of the Adoption of Automated Teller Machines. The RAND Journal of Economics, 26(3), pp. 479.
- Samantha, O. (2011). Fostering solar water heating: Policy experiences and lessons from South Africa and Tunisia. Diffusion of renewable energy technologies: Case studies of enabling frameworks in developing countries. UNEP Risø Centre on Energy, Climate and Sustainable Development, pp. 3-31.
- Sathyanarayana, S., and R. Ganesh. (2008). Rural Retail Management. Journal of Contemporary Research in Management, 7, pp. 81-99.
- Schalock, R. L. (2000). Three Decades of Quality of Life. Focus on Autism and Other Developmental Disabilities, 15(2), pp. 116–127.

- Schlegelmilch, B. , Arizona, B., Bohlen, G. & Diamantopoulos, A. The link between green purchasing decisions and measures of environmental consciousness. European Journal of Marketing, 1996, Vol. 30(5), pp. 35-55.
- Schiffman and Kanuk. Consumer Behaviour : A European Outlook. 2nd Edition, (1998).
- Schweizer-Ries, P. (2008). Energy sustainable communities: Environmental psychological investigations. Energy Policy, 36(11), pp. 4126–4135.
- Sahal, D. (1981). Alternative conceptions of technology. Research Policy, 10(1), pp. 2–24.
- Selco Foundation and Renewable Energy Working Group (REWG) (2012). Ecosystem Creation for Off-Grid Solar: Achieving Diffusion Across India. pp. 1-10.
- Sekabira, H., B. Bonabana., and N. Asingwire. (2012). Determinants for adoption of information and communications technology (ICT)-based market information services by smallholder farmers and traders in Mayuge District, Uganda. Journal of Development and Agricultural Economics, 4(14), pp. 404-415.
- Shahnaei, S. (2012). The relationship between demographic characteristics and green purchasing of Malaysian consumers.Interdisciplinary. Journal of Contemporary Research in Business, 4 (3), pp. 234 - 251.
- Shin, D. C. (1979). The Concept of Quality of Life and the Evaluation of Developmental Effort: Some Applications to South Korea. Comparative Politics, 11(3), pp. 299.
- Silva, C.E. (2008). Factors Influencing the Development of Local Renewable Energy Strategies : The cases of Lolland and Samsø Islands in Denmark.

- Smith, K. R. (2000). Indoor air pollution in developing countries and acute lower respiratory infections in children. Thorax, 55(6), pp. 518–532.
- Smith, P., (2015). Is your diesel pump costing you money? Retrieved from http://www.dpi.nsw.gov.au/__data/assets/pdf_file/0004/165217/is-your-diesel-pump-costing-you-money.pdf
- Sovacool, B. K. (2012). The political economy of energy poverty: A review of key challenges. Energy for Sustainable Development, 16(3), pp. 272–282.
- Sunil Geddam, G. Kumaravel Dinesh, Thirugnanasambandam Sivasankar, "Determination of thermal performance of a box type solar cooker", Solar Energy, vol. 113, (2015), pp.324–331.
- Sung, B., & Park, S.-D. (2018). Who Drives the Transition to a Renewable-Energy Economy? Multi-Actor Perspective on Social Innovation. Sustainability, 10(2), pp. 448.
- Suurs, R.A.A. (2009). Motors of sustainable innovation: Towards a theory on the dynamics of technological innovation systems. Unpublished doctoral dissertation. University of Utrecht, Utrecht.
- Tanuwidjaja, E (2006). Technology Diffusion: The Case of Information and Communication Technologies. New York: Oxford University Press.
- Tarde, G. The Laws of Imitation. trans. by Elsie Clews Parsons. New York: Holt; Chicago : University of Chicago Press. GS(E), (1903), (1969).
- Tawney, L., Miller, M., & Bazilian, M. (2013). Innovation for sustainable energy from a pro-poor perspective. Climate Policy, 15(1), pp.146–162.

- TISS (2013). Impact Assessment of a project on Solar Lanterns under the Aegis of Light a Billion Lives. Prepared for The Power Finance Corporation. Tata Institute of Social Studies, Mumbai.
- Taylor, S., & Todd, P. (1995). An Integrated Model of Waste Management Behaviour. Environment and Behavior, 27(5), pp. 603–630.
- Tilikidou, I. and Delistavrou, A. (2001). Utilization of Selected Demographics and Psychographics in Recycling Behavior Understanding: A Focus on Materialism. Greener Management International Journal, Issue 34, Summer, pp. 75-93.
- Tiwari, G. N., & Mishra, R. K. (2011). Advanced Renewable Energy Sources. Cambridge: Royal Society of Chemistry.
- Tornatzky, L. G., & Klein, K. J. (1982). Innovation characteristics and innovation adoption-implementation: A meta-analysis of findings. IEEE Transactions on Engineering Management, EM-29(1), pp. 28–45.
- Tollefson, J. (2019). The hard truths of climate change — by the numbers. Nature, 573(7774), pp. 324–327.
- UNDP. (2011). Universal Energy Access. Available at < http:// www. undp. org/ content/undp/en/home/ librarypage/results/fast_facts/ fast_facts_universalenergyaccess.html>
- UN. Transforming Our World: The 2030 Agenda for Sustainable Development. New York, United Nations, pp.1-29, (2015). Retrieved from https://sustainable development.un.org/post2015/transformingourworld
- Urmee, T., Harries, D., & Holtorf, H.-G. (2016). Photovoltaics for Rural Electrification in Developing Countries. Green Energy and Technology.

- Vasanath N., Akash G., Srikanth KR., Pavan, S, TN and Sinha R. Solar Powered Automatic Pesticide Sprayer. Internal Conference on Energy, Communication, Data Analytic and Soft Computing, 2017, pp. 3438-3440.
- Vaghela, L. (1993). A Study of Non- conventional Energy Devices in Rural Areas of Surat District (Gujarat), pp. 134-145.
- Venkatesh, V., & Davis, F. D. (1996). A Model of the Antecedents of Perceived Ease of Use: Development and Test. Decision Sciences, 27(3), pp. 451–481.
- Weinthal, E. (2015). Gallagher, Kelly Sims. 2014. The Globalization of Clean Energy Technology: Lessons from China. Cambridge, MA: The MIT Press. Global Environmental Politics, 15(2), pp. 150–151.
- Wieczorek, A. J., Negro, S. O., Harmsen, R., Heimeriks, G. J., Luo, L., & Hekkert, M. P. (2013). A review of the European offshore wind innovation system. Renewable and Sustainable Energy Reviews, 26, pp. 294–306.
- Wieczorek, A. J., & Hekkert, M. P. (2012). Systemic instruments for systemic innovation problems: A framework for policy makers and innovation scholars. Science and Public Policy, 39(1), pp. 74–87.
- Windrum, P., and de. Berranger, P. (2002). The Adoption of e-business technologies by SMEs. Paper presented at MERIT-Infonomics Research Memorandum series. New York, NY.
- The world health report 2002 - Reducing Risks, Promoting Healthy Life. (2013, July 29). Retrieved from https://www.who.int/whr/2002/en/
- WBCSD (World Business Council for Sustainable Development), (2010). Enabling frameworks for technology diffusion: A business perspective (Geneva: WBCSD).

- World Bank Group (2010). Addressing the Electricity Access Gap: Background Paper. World Bank Energy Sector Strategy. Retrieved from http:// siteresources. worldbank.org/EXTESC/Resources/ Addressing_the_Electricity_Access_Gap. pdf
- Yallapa, D., Vijaykumar P., Veerangouda M., and Sushilendra. Development and Evaluation of Solar powered Sprayer with Multipurpose Application. Global Humanitarian Technology Conference, 2016, pp. 1-5.
- Yaqoot, M., Diwan, P., & Kandpal, T. C. (2016). Review of barriers to the dissemination of decentralized renewable energy systems. Renewable and Sustainable Energy Reviews, 58, pp. 477–490.
- Yu, Y., Liu, J., Wang, H., & Liu, M. (2011). Assess the potential of solar irrigation systems for sustaining pasture lands in arid regions – A case study in Northwestern China. Applied Energy, 88(9), pp. 3176–3182
- Zeleke Ademe and Sameer Hameer, "Design, construction and performance evaluation of a Box type solar cooker with a glazing wiper mechanism", AIMS Energy, vol.6, (2018), pp.146-169.
- Zhang, J.J., & Morawska, L. (2002). Combustion sources of particles: 2. Emission factors and measurement methods. Chemosphere, 49(9), pp. 1059–1074.
- ZuraidahRamly, N. H. (2012). Environmentally Conscious Behavior among Malaysian Consumers:An Empirical Analysis. Jurnal Pengurusan (35), pp.111-121.
- Orgi. (n.d.). SRS Statistical Report 2016. Retrieved from http:// www. censusindia. gov.in/vital_statistics/ SRS_Reports__2016.html.

- Teaching Methods: Traditional Vs Modern (2017). (n.d.). Retrieved from https://www.stephenperse.com/blog/?pid=5&nid=45&storyid=4728
- The Merriam-Webster.com Dictionary, Merriam-Webster Inc., https://www.merriam-webster.com/dictionary/quality%20of%20life. Accessed on 12 December 2019.
- REN21. (n.d.). RENEWABLES 2018 GLOBAL STATUS REPORT. Retrieved from http://www.ren21.net/gsr-2018/
- REN21. (n.d.). RENEWABLES 2019 GLOBAL STATUS REPORT. Retrieved from https://www.ren21.net/gsr-2019/
- (n.d.). Retrieved from https://www.ibef.org/download/Power-July-2018.pdf
- (n.d.). Retrieved from https://shaktifoundation.in/wp-content/ uploads/ 2017/ 12/ Report_Renewables-India-2017-1.pdf
- (n.d.). Retrieved from http://petroleum.nic.in/sites/default/files/ipngstat_0.pdf
- (n.d.). Retrieved from http://pib.nic.in/newsite/PrintRelease.aspx?relid=174832
- (n.d.). Retrieved from http://www.oecd.org/sdd/47917288.pdf
- (n.d.). Retrieved from http://www.pib.nic.in/Pressreleaseshare.aspx?PRID=1555373
- (n.d.). Retrieved from http:// www. cea. nic. in/ reports/ monthly/ installedcapacity/ 2017/ installed capacity-02.pdf
- (n.d.). Retrieved from https://www.thecleannetwork.org/wp-content/ uploads/ 2018/ 10/ State-of-the-Decentralised-Renewable-Energy-Sector-2018.pdf

- (n.d.). Retrieved from http://hdr.undp.org/en/content/human-development-report-2001
- (n.d.). Retrieved from http:// hdr. undp.org/ sites/ default/ files/ reports/ 258/hdr _ 1997_en_complete_nostats.pdf
- (n.d.). Retrieved from https://in.one.un.org/page/sustainable-development-goals/sdg-7/
- (n.d.). Retrieved from https:// www. Undp .org/ content/ dam/ aplaws/ publication/ en/ publications/ capacity-development/capacity-development-a-undpprimer/ CDG_ PrimerReport_final_web.pdf
- (n.d.).Retrieved from https:// pmstudycircle. Com / 2012/ 03/ stakeholders-in-project-management-definition-and-types/
- (n.d.). Retrieved from https:// agriodisha. nic.in/ content/ pdf/ ACTIVITY% 20 REPORT%202017-18%20F.pdf
- (n.d.). Retrieved from https://www.bp.com/content/ dam/bp/business-sites/ en/ global/ corporate/pdfs/ energy-economics/statistical-review/bp-stats-review-2019-full-report.pdf
- (n.d.). Retrieved from http:// www. cea.nic.in/ reports/ others/ planning/ pdm/growth_ 2019.pdf
- (n.d.). Retrieved from https://mnre.gov.in/sites/ default/files schemes benchmark % 20 Order%20FY% 202019-20. pdf
- (n.d.). Retrieved from https://mnre.gov.in/file-manager/annual-report/2017-2018/ EN/ pdf/ chapter-4.pdf.
- (n.d.). Retrieved from http://www.irena.org/ newsroom/pressreleases/2018/Apr/Global-Renewable-Generation-Continues-its-Strong-Growth-New-IRENA-Capacity-Data-Shows

REFERENCES

- OVERVIEW - Ministry of New and Renewable Energy. (n.d.). Retrieved from https:// mnre.gov.in/file-manager/annual-report/2016-2017/E
- (n.d.). Retrieved from https://www.ibef.org/industry/renewable-energy/showcase
- (n.d.). Retrieved from https://inc42.com/features/30-cleantech-startups-that-offer-sustainable-lifeways-without-compromising-on-growth/
- (n.d.). Retrieved from https://www.renewableenergyworld.com/baseload/40-companies-organizations-bringing-solar-power-to-the-developing-world/#gref
- (n.d.). Retrieved from https://www.investopedia.com/investing/top-alternative-energy-companies/
- (n.d.). Retrieved from https://www.irena.org/
- (n.d.). Retrieved from https://www.valuer.ai/blog/top-10-renewable-energy-startups-list
- (n.d.). Retrieved from https://explodingtopics.com/blog/renewable-energy-startups
- (n.d.). Retrieved from https://selco-india.com/wp-
- content/uploads/2021/04/livelihoods.pdf

Glossary Of Abbreviations Used

- AC : Alternative Current
- ACECC : Advisory Group on Energy and Climate Change
- ADEME : Agence de l' Environnement et de la Maitrise de l' Energie
- AD : Accelerated Depreciation
- AEP : Auroville Energy Products
- AGECC : Advisory Group on Energy and Climate Change
- Ah : Ampere Hour
- AIDA : Awareness-Interest-Desire-Action
- ALCC : Annualised Life Cycle
- AmP : Ampere
- ATM : Automated Teller Machine
- BDO : Block Development Office
- BGL : Bhagyanagar Gas Limited
- BoP : Bottom of Pyramid
- BP : British Petroleum
- BPL : Below Poverty Line
- BU : Billion Units
- Bt : Billion Ton
- CAGR : Compound Annual Growth Rate
- CEA : Central Electricity Authority
- CEE : Clean Energy Entrepreneur
- CFA : Central Financial Assistance
- CFL : Compact Fluorescent Lamp
- CH4 : Methane
- CNG : Compressed Natural Gas
- CNC : Computer Numerical Control

- CO : Carbon Monoxide
- CO2 : Carbon Dioxide
- CPCB : Central Pollution Control Board
- CSP : Concentrated Solar Power
- CSP : Community Service Provider
- CSR : Corporate Social Responsibility
- CUTM : Centurion University of Technology and Management
- DC : Direct Current
- DDUGJY : Deen Dayal Upadhyaya Gram Jyoti Yojana
- DISCOM : Distribution Company
- DNES : Department of Non-Conventional Energy Sources
- DPR : Detailed Project Report
- DSC : Digital Service Centre
- EMI : Equated Monthly Instalment
- EVMS : Electronic Vehicle Management Systems
- FGD : Focused Group Discussion
- FIFO : First in First Out System
- FMCG : Fast Moving Consumer Goods
- GAIL : Gas Authority of India Limited
- GARV : Grameen Vidyutikaran
- GBI : Generation Based Incentive
- GDP : Gross Domestic Product
- GEC : Green Energy Corridor
- GEDCOL : Green Energy Development Corporation of Odisha
- GHG : Green House Gas
- GoI : Government of India
- GP : Gram Panchayat
- GRIDCO : Grid Corporation of Odisha
- GST : Goods and Service Tax
- GW : Gigawatt

- GWh : Gigawatt hours
- g/h : Gram/hour
- HDI : Human Development Index
- HPCL : Hindustan Petroleum Corporation Limited
- hp : Horse Power
- IBEF : India Brand Equity Foundation
- ICT : Information and Communication Tool
- IDBI : Industries Development Bank of India
- IDCO : Industry Development Corporation of Odisha
- IEA : International Energy Agency
- IEEJ : The Institute of Energy Economics Japan
- IFC : Indian Finance Corporation
- IFC : International Finance Corporation
- IFFCO : Indian Farmers Fertiliser Cooperative
- IIT : Indian Institute of Technology
- IPCC : Intergovernmental Panel on Climate Change
- IPICOL : Industrial Promotion and Investment Corporation of Odisha Limited
- IREDA : Indian Renewable Energy Development Agency Limited
- IRENA : International Renewable Energy Agency
- ISR : Individual Social Responsibility
- ISTS : Inter State Transmission System
- IT : Information Technology
- J : Joule
- J/s : Joule/second
- JLG : Joint Liability Group
- JNNSM : Jawaharlal Nehru National Solar Mission
- KPMG : Klynveld Peat Marwick Goerdeler
- KUSUM : Kisan Urja Suraksha Evan Utthan Mahaabhiyan
- kgoe : Kilogram of Oil Equivalent
- kV : Kilo Volt

- kW : Kilo Watt
- kWh : Kilo Watt Hour
- l : Litre
- LED : Light Emitting Diode
- l/h : Litre/hour
- lm : Lumens
- lm/W : Lumens/Watt
- LPG : Liquified Petroleum Gas
- m : Meter
- mAh : Milli Ampere Hour
- MEDP : Micro-Enterprise Development Programme
- MFI : Micro Finance Institutions
- MJ : Mega Joule
- MNRE : Ministry for New and Renewable Energy
- MoEF : Ministry of Environment and Forests
- MoP : Ministry of Power
- MPNG : Ministry of Petroleum and Natural Gas
- MRP : Maximum Retail Price
- MSW : Municipal Solid Waste
- Mt : Metric Ton
- MU : Million Units
- Mw : Mega Watt
- N2O : Nitrous Oxide
- NABARD : National Bank for Agricultural and Rural Development
- NAPCC : National Action Plan on Climate Change
- NBCP : National Biomass Cook Stoves Program
- NBFC : Non-Banking Financial Company
- NBMMP : National Biomass and Manure Management Program
- NCAER : National Council for Applied Economic Research
- NCEF : National Clean Energy Fund

- NEP : National Energy Policy
- NGO : Non-Government Organisations
- NiMH : Nickel–Metal Hydride
- NISE : National Institute of Solar Energy
- NITI Aayog : National Institution for Transforming India Aayog
- NIWE : National Institute of Wind Energy
- NOx : Nitrogen Oxides
- NPIC : National Program for Improved Chulha
- NREP : National Rural Electrification Policy
- NSM : National Solar Mission
- NSSO : National Sample Survey Office
- NVVN : NTPC Vidyut Vyapar Nigam
- OECD : Organisation for Economic Co-operation and Development
- OREDA : Odisha Renewable Energy Development Agency
- OREDF : Odisha Renewable Energy Development
- OHPC : Odisha Hydro Power Corporation Limited
- PACS : Pataneswari Agricultural Cooperative Society
- PDS : Public Distribution System
- PM : Project Management
- PMCL : Prime Minister's Council on Climate Change
- PMUY : Pradhan Mantri Ujjwala Yojana
- PNG : Piped Natural Gas
- PPAC : Petroleum Planning and Analysis Cell Report
- PPP : Public Private Partnership
- PPT : Power Point Presentation
- PSHS : Pico Solar Home Systems
- PPP : Purchasing Power Parity
- PV : Photo Voltaic
- QOL : Quality of Life
- RBI : Reserve Bank of India

- REC : Renewable Energy Certificate
- REWG : Renewable Energy Working Group
- RET : Renewable Energy Technology
- R&D : Research and Development
- RGGLVY : Rajiv Gandhi Grameen LPG Vitaran Yojana
- RGGY : Rajiv Gandhi Grameen Vidyutikaran Yojana
- RICE : Research Institute for Compassionate Economics
- RPO : Renewable Purchase Obligation
- RPSSGP : Roof Top PV and Small Solar Power Generation Program
- s : Second
- SBI : State Bank of India
- SCF : Standard Cubic Feet
- SEB : State Electricity Boards
- SELCO : Solar Electric Light Company
- SERC : State Electricity Regulatory Commission
- SHG : Self-Help Group
- SHS : Solar Home System
- SIDBI : Small Industries Development Bank of India
- SNA : State Nodal Agency
- SO2 : Sulphur Dioxide
- SoUL : Solar Urja Lamp
- SPM : Suspended Particulate Matter
- SRS : Sample Registration System
- SSS-NIRE : Sardar Swaran Singh National Institute of Renewable Energy
- t : Ton
- TAM : Technology Acceptance Model
- TERI : The Energy and Resources Institute
- TISS : Tata Institute of Social Sciences
- TPB : Theory of Planned Behaviour
- TRA : Theory of Reasoned Action
- UN : United Nations

- UNDP : United Nations Development Program
- UNFCCC : United Nations Climate Change
- UT : Union Territory
- V : Voltage
- VAT : Value Added Tax
- VCESPC : Village Clean Energy Service Provider Committee
- VGF : Viability Gap Funding
- VIEWS : Voluntary Integration for Education and Welfare of Society
- W : Watt
- WWW : World Wide Web
- WBCSD : World Business Council for Sustainable Development
- Wp : Watt Power
- WWF : World Wildlife Fund